Guided Meditation
and the Teaching of Jesus

Guided Meditation
and the Teaching of Jesus

Joan Cooper

Element Books

© Joan Cooper 1982
First published in Great Britain 1982 by
Element Books Limited
Longmead, Shaftesbury, Dorset

Second impression 1985

Printed in Great Britain by
Billings, Hylton Road, Worcester

Back cover photography by Maurice Slingsby
Text and cover design by Humphrey Stone

Biblical quotations are taken from
The New English Bible, Second Edition, © 1970,
by permission of Oxford and Cambridge
University Presses.

For details of the Culbone Community Trust
please write to: Mrs Rachel Greenhalgh,
Laburnum Cottage, Parracombe,
Barnstaple, N. Devon

Contents

INTRODUCTION 9

A definition of 'guided meditation', and the ways in which it is related to an experience of 'The Kingdom of Heaven'.

I. GROWTH 11

The possibility of growth depends on a recognition of an initial spiritual poverty, together with a trust in the power that can make growth possible – meditation on the individual personality experienced as rooms in a house – the gradual fading away of the old self – meditation on the effects of Jesus' teaching on personal relationships – the need for a time of stillness each day – meditation on the Lord's Prayer – the four great needs expressed in that prayer.

2. THE JOURNEY 24

The spiritual journey into light and truth expressed through the image of a sea voyage – the need for a trusted guide or pilot – meditation on the experience of casting outworn values into the ocean – why there is no rejection or shame if this proves impossible at the moment – the possibility of serving both God and mammon – the need for gentleness with ourselves as well as with other people – the journey dependant on our trust in Christ, who can guide us to our higher selves without usurping our will – as the trust grows the anxieties of the old self fade away – meditation centred on a garden and based on Christ's invitation to ask, seek and knock – the visible and invisible results of our seeking – our burdens are the parts of ourselves which do not wish to grow – meditation experience to increase our non-judgemental understanding of other people – the danger of secret judgements – the way lightened by the finding of many small treasures each day leading to the 'Pearl of Great Price' – meditation on discoveries to be made in a garden – the lesson of trust to be learnt from Christ's walking on the water – meditation based on this and on the experience of making a journey as a young child.

3. THE SEED 45

Meditation on the parable of the sower – the different grounds of each individual – the experience of the growing processes of a plant – meditation on the various factors that inhibit plant growth – the plant's need for a gardener – the difficulty of asking help from anyone on the physical plane – the shift from head centring to heart centring – *giving and caring for other people in a sensitive response to their needs – meditation on the experience of an orchard giving its fruits – the gift of ourselves – reflections on the wages of giving and the parable of the workers in the vineyard – the growth that comes from giving.*

4. THE POWER OF JESUS 61

Reflections on the raising of Jairus' daughter – the spiritual power of meditation – meditation on the experience of leaving a prison cell or any place of bondage – the keys that open the door to the Kingdom of Heaven – Christ's power of caring and healing – the vibrations we all give out – the image of the caring, spiritual family, and the restrictions of biological family units – meditation on the growth of individuality, and the different aspects of ourselves – Christ as the gardener – meditation on different parts of a garden – the need to let some parts of ourselves die in order to transform stumbling blocks into assets – meditation on the experience of shedding burdens as we make our spiritual journey – the importance of relationships.

5. THE SUBSTANCE OF LIFE 76

Reflections on the feeding of the five thousand – the 'miracle' of spiritual food feeding the physical body – the nature of giving from the heart – Christ's act of giving – everyone's power of giving – the distinction between 'miracle' and magic – our dependance on 'the living water' and on spiritual 'meat and drink'.

Joan Cooper died at the height of her work and this book contains the essence of her teaching.

All her friends and students are happy that through this book they may share the love and wisdom that she offered so freely. Her work is being continued by the Culbone Community Trust.

Introduction

This book is about the way in which Jesus taught his friends, by giving them actual experience of another kind of thinking and being which already existed as *potential* within them, but had not yet been realised. He used *place* as a concept to denote the quality of experience of which a person was capable at a given time; he used *place* to describe the level of being which a person inhabited and from which he thought and acted. The place called 'earth' was the place within the person from which he habitually acted or thought; the place called 'the kingdom of heaven' was the new, higher level of being to which a person could attain and within which he would have a new outlook, new understanding, new experience of himself and other people and the world around him. Jesus taught in such a way as to give his friends experience of this new state or level of being which he called 'the kingdom of heaven'.

This book is based on my own experience of the way in which Jesus taught, which is a method used today by some people in the teaching of meditation and called 'guided meditation'. 'Guided meditation' can mean anything and lead people in many different directions because the guidance depends upon the teacher. It is simply a method by which the pupil is more or less passively led (i.e., without using his own imagination and letting images come into his mind) by the teacher's words to the place or experience the teacher desires for him. There can be any kind of principle or motive behind this exercise. My own study of the Gospels has given me an *interior* experience of how and what Jesus taught which reveals an extensive use of so-called 'guided meditation'. My personal experience is of a Jesus who rarely preached but whose teaching was focussed on giving people new experiences of themselves – new experiences beyond themselves as they were and as they thought of themselves. My own experience is of a Jesus who gave people actual experiences of the kind of spiritual growth which was possible for them and so increased in them the longing for this growth.

This book is about the meditations which I believe Jesus used and the kinds of experience which they would provide. I have selected from all four Gospels to illustrate his teaching. In some instances there will be conflict between the meditation-experiences, as I understand them, and how the relevant Gospel passages are usually interpreted. The reader will have to consider this conflict and decide for himself whether or not to reject my personal experience – and hence interpretation – of the relevant passage. This particular book is NOT about this conflict, nor is it directly concerned with the truth or falsity of different statements in the Gospels. Nonetheless, this book could not be written without implied – and sometimes explicit – criticism of certain statements made in the Gospels which I believe from my own experience to be a direct contradiction of what Jesus taught. The reader is asked only to accept that this is my own experience, for which I offer neither testimony nor apology, and to listen within his own interior self as to whether or not it has the ring of truth. . . .

1. Growth

All growth begins with a recognition of need. One could almost say this of plant life. The seed 'needs' to recognise its poverty as a seed before it can desire to grow into a plant. Without this 'need' the seed could not die to being a seed and risk sending forth its tender and vulnerable shoot into the darkness of the soil. Once it starts the journey up through the dark soil, there is no turning back; the safe shell of the seed disintegrates – dies. The impetus must be sufficiently strong; the desire to grow has to carry the shoot forward until it breaks ground and becomes a plant. Equally import-ant is the vision of what is possible. The seed needs to have, locked up within itself, some picture of what is possible: of what it can become. And finally, within that will-to-grow, inherent in the seed, is the knowledge that such growth is possible.

On human scale, the knowledge that spiritual growth is possible expands and becomes what we call 'trust'. Trust is an expression of the knowledge that there is Someone and some Power that make our growth possible. Jesus came to give people an experience of their inner potential, of what was possible for them to grow into. The Gospels contain a pale reflection of the actual meditation experiences through which he led his friends so that they could reach out, briefly, to their own potentials and return with a clear vision of what they could then begin to grow towards. His teaching commenced with enabling people to experience their own needs, by recognising the poverty of themselves as they were and how, out of poverty, could come the new growth: the new perception, the new knowledge, the new experi-ence and understanding, the new relationship to God. This teaching is expressed in a preacherly way in the first part of the Sermon on the Mount, in some of what are called the Beatitudes. (Matthew v, 3-8) This is how Jesus taught the truths contained in these verses, in a form inspired to give his friends experiences of themselves, of that inner poverty or need which alone could lead them to a new level of growth in themselves. This form is altered slightly here to enable the twentieth century person to follow the meditation.

MEDITATION-EXPERIENCE

Visualise a house (a simple Mediterranean house with a ground floor, first floor, flat roof . . . and white-washed). There are two halves to this house and the door is in the middle. . . . In your mind walk up to the door of the house . . . open it . . . walk in . . . and turn to the right. The rooms of the ground floor are full of possessions . . . your own possessions. Experience your satisfaction and pleasure in these possessions. Experience a sensation of self-assurance and confidence through having possessions. . . . Now go up to the first floor . . . and experience here the fullness of your own mental possessions . . . your practical skills that enable you to live your life . . . the knowledge you have gained from the different kinds of experience you have had . . . your intellectual knowledge – maybe there is a library full of books. . . . Experience, as far as you can, the completeness of all your *knowing* as it exists now . . . and include those intimations of intuitive knowledge which indicate deeper levels of spiritual awareness and knowledge which belong to your innermost being. . . . Experience how your mind-possessions, together with your material possessions, give you the feeling of your own identity. . . . There is also a temple – chapel – somewhere in this part of the house . . . it may be only a corner of a room. . . . Experience this place which contains your religious beliefs . . . the *rightness* for which you strive. . . . Experience the principles that make your life and you seem right – and even sometimes righteous. . . . Experience also the feelings of guilt that refer to the unattainableness of this structure of principle and rightness. . . .

Now, go back to the front door of this house and stand inside, with your back to it, experiencing the entire section of house you have just visited. . . . Do you experience that it is complete in itself? . . . Do you experience its lack of space? How nothing new can enter into it . . . because there is no room? Do you experience confinement and a kind of airlessness or suffocation in this part of the house? Or are you satisfied with it as it is? . . . If you are satisfied with this section of the house as it is . . . as you have experienced it . . . conclude the meditation by leaving the house, shutting the door behind you, and returning to an awareness of your physical body and the position in which it is sitting.

If you experience a lack of space in the section of house you have visited . . . or any sense of being confined by it . . . go into the other side of the house. On the ground floor you will find one room only. It is completely empty. Experience its bareness . . . the shock of its bareness . . . Experience its poverty . . . and of how you feel without the confidence and security of possessions. . . . Experience this bareness in yourself . . . a part of yourself you do not normally inhabit. . . . Now, move to one of the windows and look out. Observe all the manifestations of nature that are visible to you . . . the earth and the plants and trees that are near at hand . . . and everything at a distance, even to the skyline. Observe the abundance of nature's expression: its colour and form and fragrance. Look at the sky . . . and its reflection of light . . . even from the formations of cloud cover. Open yourself to everything you can see from that window . . . and know it is yours to feed upon. Experience the nourishment which it supplies to your innermost being. . . . (Matthew v, 5)

Now, observe people passing by your window . . . or in the distance . . . and experience compassion and understanding for them as you stand in this bare part of the house . . . naked and without the inhibiting barriers which possessions and self-confidence give you. Experience your sensitivity and vulnerability as you watch the people passing . . . of your need for them . . . and of the feeling of *caring* which flows from mutual need. . . . (Matthew v, 7)

Now, experience your own spiritual needs . . . whatever real spiritual need you can sense in yourself in this bare room, where you are exposed to yourself and cannot hide behind possessions. . . . Experience the comfort flowing into you, from nowhere in particular, unimpeded, to answer your need. . . . (Matthew v, 4)

Now, go upstairs to the single room above . . . and observe that it also appears to be bare. . . . Experience the emptiness in your mind. . . . Experience your own ignorance . . . and not-knowing. . . . (Matthew v, 3) Now, experience the desire in yourself to be filled with *real* knowledge . . . with the truth. . . . (Matthew v, 6) Observe a ladder in the corner of the room that leads onto the roof . . . and experience, as you move towards that ladder, your own heart's deepest desire . . . which is to know God. . . . (Matthew v, 8) Now, climb that ladder . . . out of your need and your desire . . . and find on the roof the nourishment . . . truth . . . vision you most need. . . .

After a time, return down the ladder . . . go back down the stairs to the front door. Pause at the front door and decide which side of this house you will light up for other people to see . . . and be invited into . . . in order to experience what you personally have learned. . . . (Matthew v, 14–16) Then, come out of the house . . . shut the door . . . and return very slowly to a physical awareness of where you are actually sitting.

The house is an ancient symbol of man and the different parts of his being, each level representing some aspect of his mind. Many meditation experiences are possible, based on this symbolic house, and can reveal different kinds of things to us, according to the aim of the meditation and what each of us is capable of experiencing. The ground floor represents, generally speaking, our practical relationships to life and our skills; the first floor stands for different kinds of knowledge, both intellectual and intuitive, as well as the acquired attitudes which influence our thinking about ourself and our life. A top floor or roof represents the place from which we receive inspiration, guidance, vision.

This meditation speaks for itself. It enables us to experience both our fullness and our emptiness, the part of ourself which is weak or poor that we usually hide from acknowledging. The experience can be – according to each person's desire to know – one of realising that fullness/righteousness cannot go beyond itself, whereas from the weak/empty part of ourself growth can take place and new experience is possible. This is the essence of the teaching contained in these verses. All things are possible for the person who is able to recognise and accept his emptiness, his lack, his need; he will be nourished and given understanding, he will experience compassion for others, he will have a vision of his own spiritual path.

How do we grow spiritually? What does it feel like – and how is it different from what we have been doing all along? Is it not merely an extension of what we already are – an improvement on our character that is already striving to live up to a code of behaviour: to live in accordance with The Law? When a person has become aware of his own need, discovered the emptiness in himself, and experienced a longing for spiritual growth – what happens? Does he clear out his possessions in the other part of the house – metaphorically speaking? Does he throw away the books in his library and get rid of those acquired attitudes that have tightly structured his life and which he has tried to live up to for years? In his initial enthusiasm he is all for making a clean start.

Jesus speaks to this person in us: 'Do not suppose that I have come to abolish the Law and the prophets; I did not come to abolish, but to complete'. (Matthew v, 17) But if we are not to clear out and get rid of, in order to make a new beginning, what are we to do? There seem to be gaps in the actual teaching, but indications are given that nothing should be altered by abolishing; instead, new growth – a new understanding – commences in another part of ourselves. The stern moral code of the Law belongs to one part of our being; it forms part of the rigid social structure within which we live our physical life on earth. That part can remain undisturbed, for it will fade away naturally when the new part – the growing part of us – becomes strong in its new understanding. This new understanding is contrasted with the old structure in verses 38 to 42:

> You have learned that they were told, 'An eye for an eye, and a tooth for a tooth.' But what I tell you is this: Do not set yourself against the man who wrongs you. If someone slaps you on the right cheek, turn and offer him your left. If a man wants to sue you for your shirt, let him have your coat as well. If a man in authority makes you go one mile, go with him two. Give when you are asked to give; and do not turn your back on a man who wants to borrow.

And in verses 43 to 45:

> You have learned that they were told, 'Love your neighbour, hate your enemy.' But what I tell you is this: Love your enemies and pray for your persecutors; only so can you be children of your heavenly Father. . . .

In this new place in ourself, we can behave differently. This is not behaviour related to a moral code, it is not a kind of striving to be 'good'. It is a *natural* response from this new place – the empty place in us; it comes from the heart rather than from the head.

The following meditation framework is one which can be used today to enable us to experience what Jesus meant in the above verses. Its effectiveness on any one occasion will depend upon both teacher and pupil and the depth of their desires to experience truth.

Growth

First of all take the necessary steps to prepare for meditation. Sit comfortably, relaxing your body as far as possible. Close your eyes and let the tensions drain away from the small muscles of the face. Relax the top of the head and allow any thoughts to drift away. Sit for a few minutes just listening, letting any audible sounds flow through your mind.

Now, let your mind be taken back to Palestine . . . and receive an impression of Jesus walking around the Sea of Galilee, finding disciples. . . . Allow pictures or sensations of some kind to come into your mind. . . . Wait to receive whatever can be given to you. . . . Now, you will hold in your mind the thought that you are going to visit the household of John, James, and their father, Zebedee. Hold the thought . . . but do not imagine anything. Some picture or sensation will be presented to you . . . if you wait patiently. . . . The first impression you will be given will be of the household of Zebedee as it was when Jesus met John and James. Experience this household and the order or structure of life in it at that time . . . and how it depended upon strict observance of the Jewish Law. . . . Allow yourself to experience as much of the structure of this way of life . . . and in as wide a variety of ways . . . as you can. . . . Someone from outside offends a member of the household. Observe . . . experience . . . the reaction. . . . Observe . . . experience . . . how the household gives to a neighbour in need. . . . Observe . . . experience . . . the striving to live up to the moral code. . . .

Now, let this picture slowly fade . . . and visit the same household two years later. . . . Again, allow yourself to experience the order and structure of life in this household . . . two years after James and John had become intimate friends of Jesus. . . . Observe . . . experience . . . the difference (if any) in how James and John live their lives. Allow yourself, if possible, to experience the sensations that

denote the difference reflected in your own body. . . .
Observe . . . experience . . . what happens when one of them
is attacked or offended. . . . Observe . . . experience . . . how
they relate to their neighbours. . . . Observe . . . experience
. . . what has happened to the striving. . . .

Now, allow the experiences and the scene to fade from
your mind and let your awareness return to the physical
sensation of your body and its posture of sitting. Always
close the door completely on any meditation experience and
do not allow it to become confused with your daily life, or
yourself to drift in any way between the two.

It is only an experience of *need*: of poverty and emptiness
as we are and the longing to be filled with spiritual susten-
ance, that awakens in us the possibility of spiritual growth.
That is our first truth; that is our starting point. The second
truth has to do with realising that growth takes place from
this very place in ourselves which is empty, where space
exists. It hasn't anything to do with striving to live up to 'the
law' of any religious or moral code. The law – the code or
religious structure – exists in another part of ourselves; it
cannot simply be discarded. It must continue to co-exist
with the new growth, in the other part of our beings, which
is so utterly different. One day 'the law' will fade away
because it is no longer necessary, having achieved its only
true spiritual purpose in our complete renewal. Our rebirth
into new purpose and understanding and a new quality of
aliveness is the 'fulfilment of the law'.

In order to make possible this rebirth in ourselves – in
order to allow any spiritual growth to take place, we need to
make space daily in our lives, by stopping the automatic
flow of activity and withdrawing briefly to a stillness that is
both within and without. For that brief period of time it is
necessary to 'shut the door' on the busy-ness of our life and
our thoughts and allow ourselves simply to experience the
'new', the 'other', the reality of the spiritual plane which is
always present, even when we are not aware of it.

And so Jesus taught his friends at this stage to meditate

and to pray, very simply – without any kind of ritual performance being required. A pale reflection of his teaching is contained in Matthew vi, verses 9-13, in what is called 'the Lord's prayer'. The lack of understanding which led to its being presented in this way is due to some people's resistance to Jesus and his teaching. They resisted Jesus because they could not allow themselves to grow spiritually, and therefore they were not capable of understanding how spiritual growth could take place in other people. They could not even accept that this was what the teaching of Jesus was about.

This is how Jesus really took his friends through what we call 'the Lord's prayer'.

THE LORD'S PRAYER – MEDITATION AND PRAYER

When you have prepared yourself physically and mentally for meditation, taking the time you feel you need, *experience yourself* . . . as you are at this moment . . . physically, the different parts of your body . . . and mentally, with your different thoughts . . . and any intimations of desire or longing that take you beyond your present state. . . .

Now, visualise a Person who is at a higher spiritual level than yourself – this may be your spiritual teacher who is in a physical body . . . it may be a spiritual being . . . it may be a clear image you have of God. . . . This Person cares for you with all love . . . requires nothing of you . . . does not judge you . . . does not try to smother you. . . . Experience the power of this caring and love . . . which leaves you completely free. . . . Let some response flow from you . . . to this Person who cares so completely for you. . . .

Now, allow this Person . . . who cares for you personally . . . to come close to you. . . . Experience this Person's intimate presence. . . . Now, allow your own mind and being to extend towards that Person . . . to enter into that Person . . . so you experience from INSIDE the Person some quality of that Person's being . . . or character. . . .

Allow yourself to open as fully as you can . . . and to extend beyond the limitations of your ordinary self . . . into that Person. . . . Let the Person enter you . . . nourish you . . . grow you. . . . After allowing a time for this inter-penetration or union . . . withdraw slowly into your own smaller self again. . . .

When you are in your smaller self again . . . experience the desire in yourself . . . in the core of yourself . . . to expand . . . to grow . . . to evolve into the possibilities or potential of which you have just had an intimation in your experience of union . . . however shadowy that experience may have been. . . . Experience the *need* for spiritual food . . . in order to grow. . . . Experience the *need* for encouragement . . . in order to grow. . . . Experience the *need* for challenges . . . adventures . . . even tests . . . in order to grow. . . .

Experience the *need* to see clearly what is true . . . and to know what is false *for you* at this time . . . in order to grow. . . .

Experience once more the power of caring . . . of that Person for you . . . and the fulfilment of all these needs in some measure . . . by that Person. . . .

Slowly relax your concentration . . . and return to an awareness of your physical body . . . your physical sur-rounding . . . and your physical life.

This personal experience of Jesus' own teaching of 'the Lord's prayer' – which will, no doubt, come in for much criticism – shows that it was meant to be both meditation and prayer. As meditation, it is an experience of being aware, first of all, of ourself, our state, and the different parts of our being manifesting at a particular moment in time. Secondly, it leads to a direct experience of a Person – Someone whom we know, love, respect as having the integrity to teach us and to grow us. This must be someone whom we trust; but trust is not abstract, and so our ability to relate to this Person – to extend into this Person – will depend upon the depth of this trust. If the Person is the right one for us, the necessary trust will grow.

The essence of the meditation experience lies in our desire to transcend, in however limited a way, our self as it is now and enter into the Person. It requires a letting go of ourself, our limitations, the boundaries with which we define 'our identity', and allowing the will-to-grow to flow upwards, without reservations, into the Person. For a moment there is a union of ourself with the Person, in which the Person also flows into us, feeding us. These are words. They cannot describe or truly comprehend the experience. Each time, the experience will be different and the emotional intensity will vary. It is important to remember that this meditation experience is NOT about giving up ourself or letting some-one else, however high or evolved a spiritual being, take over our own being in any way. It is about letting go, momentarily, the barriers that inhibit growth and extend-ing ourself into the Person who can nourish us and grow us into WHAT WE ALREADY ARE in potential. For this reason it is important not only to learn to trust and respond to trust, so that this extension of ourself and therefore our growth can take place; it is equally important to find the Person who is right for us and whose integrity is known to us. There may be more than one such Person. There is likely to be Someone on the spiritual plane with whom it is right to perform this meditation; there may also be Someone who inhabits a physical body and who can teach and grow us in this way.

The other part of this prayer-meditation has to do with petition: with a recognition of our daily spiritual needs and asking for their fulfilment. The first need is obvious and stated clearly in the Gospels. The spiritual being can-not grow without food, any more than the physical body can grow or be maintained without its own form of nourishment. Spiritual food is, indeed, more important than physical food as Jesus illustrated later on in his teach-ing. (Matthew xv, 29-39) We can live for a time with very little physical food, but without spiritual nourishment our life is empty of meaning and a travesty.

Our second need is for encouragement. 'Forgive us our debts as we forgive our debtors' reflects the Jewish teaching about sin and people's preoccupation with their burden of sin and their need for forgiveness. Jesus knew that the greater need in us was for acceptance – an unqualified acceptance of ourselves as we are. The focus on sin and forgiveness creates in us a structure of guilt and striving and self-deception and, ultimately, a situation in which nothing can change in us because we are unable to accept ourselves as we are. God's acceptance of us as we are, without judgment or the ritual of forgiveness, is the only possible starting point for our spiritual growth. Jesus knew this, but he also knew that our spiritual need is for even more than acceptance. Our deepest need is for encouragement from the One who is spiritually above us, which is the next step that takes us beyond acceptance and being accepted along the pathway of spiritual growth.

The third need is for the kind of challenge which stimulates growth, awakens us out of torpor or sleep, and enables us to learn. We do not instinctively expose ourselves to new situations; we tend to repeat what we have already done, to coast on what we have already acquired. We are often timid about new adventures. If it were left to our habits of living and thinking we should not increase our trust in spiritual guidance and purpose because we would not seek to be challenged or put to the test. But this is our third need: to be put to the test, to be given challenges and adventures which call forth a new leap in trust, and the courage to go beyond ourselves as they are. Jesus could never have said: 'lead us not into temptation', because this statement is spiritually unsound. Once we have started our spiritual journey, challenges and tests are necessary to keep us moving. We have to recognise our need and ask for them to be given to us, in the right way and at the right time.

Our fourth need is to be able to see clearly what is true and what is false for us throughout each day, in the context of our ordinary lives. Our spiritual growth depends upon our own discrimination and the growth in us of that inner touchstone which can tell us *what is* and *how it is*. No one can take this innermost sense of Truth from us – nor can anyone usurp our need to use and develop it, not even God! It is to this inner touchstone that we must refer all things, all experiences; its growth in sensitivity and insight *is* our own spiritual growth. And so we ask not to be 'delivered from evil' but for the growth of the part within our own soul that can know what is evil or destructive for us and what is positive and true and can nourish us. Upon this discernment and its application to our daily lives depends our spiritual growth.

The prayer concludes, as it began, with a form of meditation–experience, in which we become aware of the power of love coming from the Person that can supply our needs. This is not merely an *answering* of needs, because the needs which we recognise in ourselves are not questions to be answered but hungers to be satisfied. The power of the Person – which is the power that comes from caring or love – fills the space of our hunger, nourishes the soul, stimulates the will to learn. Our awareness of this power concludes our prayer-meditation with an experience of certainty and hope.

2. The Journey

'Do not store up for yourselves treasure on earth. . . . The lamp of the body is the eye. . . . No one can serve two masters. . . .'

(MATTHEW vi, 19–24)

Jesus grew up familiar with boats – small fishing boats and larger trading vessels that worked their way around the Mediterranean and even ventured to distant lands. Many of the spiritual experiences which he gave people in the course of his teaching were based on boats and the journeys people could make in boats. His teaching was essentially about making journeys, the journeys individual souls make as they grow from one state of being to another. No experience could better describe this spiritual journey than sailing in a small boat across a lake, like the Sea of Galilee, with its challenges and risks and unexpected dangers. The meditation-experience related to these verses, through which Jesus taught his friends, is based on such a journey.

The above verses do not immediately appear to be about a journey. They contrast two different kinds of security on which we can rely and two kinds of 'master' whom we can serve. They relate to two contrasting states of being – or two very different places in ourselves. One state concerns the place called 'earth' which contains the structure of life and forms of security we have built up for ourselves and is our starting point on the spiritual path. (There is no other starting point than where we are now.) The other state is represented by the place called 'heaven' towards which we are journeying, – where a different kind of experience is possible, a different set of values exists, a different kind of 'master' is to be served. Between one state and the other lies a sea – or country – which has to be crossed, where there is all the risk of letting go the known forms and expressions of our life and allowing our innermost desire for growth to launch us into the unknown. That inner desire for truth, new experience, increased understanding is the essential condition for such a journey; but it cannot be undertaken alone, without a spiritual 'master' – without our being aware of the presence, love, power of One who can guide and encourage.

The passage in Matthew which stands between the comparison of two different states in ourselves (19–21 and v. 24) is concerned with seeing the truth of things for ourselves. What is: what is not. This is not abstract Truth or Principle, Law or Religious Code; this is about what exists – or does not exist – now, in ourselves and in our relationships to other people. 'If your eyes are sound, you will have light for your whole body.' (v. 22) The spiritual journey from the place where we are at this moment, to the new place which we cannot yet see and of which we have only vague intimations of greater light, greater capacity for understanding and love, is *only possible* through the light of truth. It is only possible if we allow truth – the little truth that is in us now – to grow in us so its lamp enables our eye to perceive *what is*. This requires courage; courage comes from the intensity of our desire to grow. But it is also based on the extent to which we can trust the Person who is with us, who guides and encourages us. Truth is the light which expands us and makes our journey possible; our journey is, in fact, a journey in truth. The journey from one shore to the other is a journey into increasing light and growing truth.

MEDITATION–EXPERIENCE

This is how Jesus taught his friends – this is the spiritual experience he gave them when they were actually on a boat, making a journey across the Sea of Galilee, from one shore to the other. It is re-worded for someone living today.

The Journey

You are going on a journey. . . . You are in a boat.
Experience being in a boat . . . on a journey. . . . Each one of
you has a large parcel. . . . Experience your own parcel. . . .
It contains things you cannot leave behind. . . . You are on
the sea . . . and the boat has moved away from the shore. . . .
It feels overladen . . . but Christ is in control. . . .

Christ now says: We cannot continue with such a load.
The boat might manage it . . . but this is a spiritual journey
. . . and the parcel you have contains parts of yourself which
belong to the place we have left behind. . . . These parts of
you have nothing to do with the place to which we are
going. You will have to open your parcels . . . and look
inside and see what is there. . . . Then you can decide
whether or not to proceed with the journey. . . .

Now, open your parcel . . . and look carefully at its
contents. . . .

Christ says: Let spiritual light shine through your eyes . . .
and see the truth about the parcel and yourself. . . . Eventually, Christ speaks again: Decide what you want. . . . Do
you want to hold onto all that is in your parcel . . . and
return to where you came from? . . . Or do you find you
have outgrown some of its contents . . . which you can
therefore jettison . . . and continue with me on the journey
. . . trusting me and your own desire for this journey?

Decide what you want . . . what you can do. . . .

If this is the core of the teaching contained in the above
verses, they take on a different meaning. There is no longer
the rigidity of two alternatives which are mutually exclusive
– no longer the impossible requirement of opting wholly for
the one and rejecting the other. The dualism of the preacher,
with its irreconcilable opposites, disappears and is replaced
by the teacher who is not so much concerned with principles and absolutes – you cannot serve two masters: – as
with human experience and the underlying spiritual realities
in which opposites co-exist and growth takes place slowly
through growing insight. How ready are you to go on a
journey? That is the question. You cannot take the whole of

your old mind with you on this journey because the other shore is a place where you will be able to think and act from a new mind. If you are really wanting this journey, some things must go; these are the parts of your mind which you have outgrown, which you no longer need. Maybe they were useful at one time, like attitudes of caution, anger, certain fears. In any case, they were natural to you – and to other people – in the one state and in the place where you are at present; various forms of security and material possessions are important at one stage and lose their relevance later on, when you have grown. There is no command here, no requirement, but simply the question: Have you outgrown them sufficiently to follow Christ and your own desire for spiritual growth to the farther shore? Or do you need more time, more experience where you are, before you can really commit yourself to the journey? There is no shame in abandoning the journey, because it *cannot* be undertaken until you are able to jettison some of the contents of your parcel. Until this happens, there is no journey – only imagination.

It is not possible to ask this question before you start on your journey. None of us can anticipate how we will feel when we are at sea, separated from the shore of familiar places and still a long distance from that unknown shore towards which we are desiring to move. On a little boat, at sea, Christ can ask us this question: What about the parcel you are carrying . . . is it out of habit? What is in it? What are you finished with . . . and can throw overboard . . . or give to me? Just see.

There is no judgment, no risk of rejection if we can't make it just yet. In this context it is impossible to pretend to ourselves or to Christ. In the meditation–experience we look into his eyes, from which truth shines out purely and clearly. No gesture – no sacrifice – is possible. He requires no sacrifice. There is only gentleness and caring – caring even if we have to go back. We do not lose him if we need to go on serving that 'other master' too for a time and learn more lessons. We can carry on serving two masters.

A parable, attributed to Jesus, is recorded in Luke's Gospel (xvi, 1-8) which explains the necessity for some people to 'go back' and carry on with their learning on the nether shore before undertaking the journey in full. This understanding does not come from the parable as it stands, although verse nine can be read as giving some insight into our need for working out the variety of desires in us – not jumping through imagination into the boat and making the journey before we are entirely prepared for it. This is how the parable reads:

> He said to his disciples, 'There was a rich man who had a bailiff, and he received complaints that this man was squandering the property. So he sent for him, and said, 'What is this that I hear? Produce your accounts, for you cannot be manager here any longer.' The bailiff said to himself, 'What am I to do now that my employer is dismissing me? I am not strong enough to dig, and too proud to beg. I know what I must do to make sure that, when I have to leave, there will be people to give me house and home.' He summoned his master's debtors one by one. To the first he said, 'How much do you owe my master?' He replied, 'A thousand gallons of olive oil.' He said, 'Here is your account. Sit down and make it five hundred; and be quick about it.' Then he said to another, 'And you, how much do you owe?' He said, 'A thousand bushels of wheat', and was told, 'Take your account and make it eight hundred.' And the master applauded the dishonest bailiff for acting so astutely. For the worldly are more astute than the other-worldly in dealing with their own kind.

Jesus gave his friends an experience of going back, after having started the journey, because they needed to work through certain aspects of themselves which they could not take with them. Only a shadow of the truth is presented in the verses above. The 'bailiff' is not wholly able to serve the 'master', i.e., the new and growing part of himself. This new part of him is not yet able to take control: it cannot 'do its job properly'. And so the person must turn his attention to those parts of himself which are represented as the 'debtors' – not debtors to the 'master' but debtors to himself. They are parts of himself which he still feels owe him something. In other words, they are parts of himself through which he *feels himself*, with which he identifies himself. He cannot cut himself off completely from them. He can 'cancel' half of what they owe him: he is half freed from needing them as much as he did; but he needs them nevertheless as a 'place to go to', as expressions of himself. The new growing part of himself – the 'master' – understands and approves of this action, because it knows that spiritual growth depends upon this temporary 'going back'.

We need to be gentle with ourselves as well as with other people and not place upon either expectations or requirements which are impossible of fulfilment. There must be a strong desire for the journey before it can be completed, and the resistance to it (in any form) must be minimal. Only a strong desire can produce the courage for such a journey and the trust in Christ necessary to take us through storms and the unpredictable. Very often we are stopped at the beginning of the journey and can go no further. That is the time when we need to know that there is a way back – the boat can turn around and go back and wait for another time. The way back needs to be kept open by us, for ourselves and for other people whom we may be helping. We may think that the person should be able to go; we may even see that the 'way back' is going to be unproductive, a way of marking time out of fear. We may see that the person has really completed all he had to on that particular plane. Nevertheless, we must allow for this to happen and we must never withdraw our support of the person – even if he is marking time and is afraid. *Our* support – as much as Christ's – keeps the way forward open to him again when he has gained sufficient strength.

The word 'gentleness' does not fully describe Christ, for in his eyes is also the *power* of love to encourage and draw us on, not out of ourselves or into any giving up of ourselves, but on into a bigger conception of ourselves. We shall be there, on that boat, with a smaller, emptier parcel, when the time is right for us individually and for our growth. In the meantime, he is not only with those who are undertaking the journey now, he is also with those of us who have returned for more experience.

The journey does not only depend upon looking at our parcel and being able to dispose of some of its contents because we have outgrown them. It also depends upon learning to trust and accept direction from Christ. The efforts needed for the journey consist of a delicate balance between what we can do ourselves to see truthfully where we are, to discard what we no longer require, to ask for help; and the necessity of trusting Christ so much that we can put ourselves in his hands to teach and to grow us. This is where a struggle ensues which goes on for a long time. We need to clarify what this struggle is about.

The independent – and even isolated – self in each one of us has evolved through many earlier stages of acquiring different kinds of possessions for ourselves. Some of these possessions may now be of a physical or material kind, but most of them are of a more subtle nature like different kinds of knowledge or skill. Even material possessions may symbolise possessions of a more subtle nature, through which we feel our own identities. As we evolve through all the stages of self-expression, we add new facets to our beings and strengthen the already formed centre of independence, pride, isolation. As our existence continues over long periods of time, before or after our physical life on earth, the desire increases in us to outgrow or transcend this stage of independence. The struggle that develops is not really a conflict between that independent part of us and the will to grow further. It is a struggle resulting from the spiritual fact that we cannot grow beyond this state unless we put ourselves wholly in the hands of a spiritual teacher whom we can love and trust to guide us on our journey, without distorting or taking over our beings. The conflict lies not only in the unwillingness of the independent self to give up its control, it lies equally in the existential fear of being taken over. Can we trust there is a power that comes from Someone's love strong enough to guide us *to ourselves*, our higher selves, and not usurp our will? There is another stage – and still another stage – within us, waiting to be grown into; we cannot grow ourselves into the stage beyond where we are now. Can we ally our will-to-grow to the love of our spiritual teacher, the love of Christ, to grow us? Can we trust enough?

Again, there is no absolute answer. There is no question of trust or not-trust. There is only the experience of growing trust – growing slowly, as seeds grow – and of diminishing un-trust. Christ, or our spiritual teacher, accepts the growing and the diminishing as realities. They are within the texture of our daily lives. This is what the last verses of the sixth chapter of Matthew are about. (v, 25-31) Anxiety comes from the independent self, the self that thinks it can go it alone. As trust grows, anxieties fall away and we become free to go on that journey where we need to live each moment and every day for itself. In this way we approach the new shore, the new stage in our being.

> Ask, and you will receive; seek, and you will find; knock, and the door will be opened. For everyone who asks receives, he who seeks finds, and to him who knocks, the door will be opened. (vii, 7-8)

Christ cannot grow us unless – or until – we reach out to him with our seeking. To seek, or to ask, opens the door of our beings so that we can receive. Unless we ask, we cannot receive. Jesus gave his friends an experience of what it meant to ask in a simple meditation that referred to a garden. In this context of plant-life and growing, the desire to seek would come naturally. This is the kind of exercise Jesus used.

MEDITATION-EXPERIENCE

Visualise . . . or let come into your mind . . . the picture of a garden. It is a walled garden . . . large, and containing a variety of shrubs . . . flowers . . . trees. . . . There are many paths . . . and people in this garden . . . and gardeners working in it. . . . You are walking about in this garden . . . experiencing its beauty and all that it can offer you. . . . As you move about in the garden . . . a question comes into your mind . . . something you most desire to know. . . . It may have to do with the garden . . . the name of a plant . . . something about how to care for it. . . . It may not seem to relate directly to the garden at all. . . . Ask your question of someone . . . and experience opening yourself to receive the answer. . . . As you walk about in the garden . . . you experience seeking something. . . . You need to find something special . . . that has meaning just for you. . . . It may not be anything big . . . it may be a tiny thing . . . but for you it will be a 'treasure' that means more than anything else in the garden . . . or it may seem to give meaning to the experience of being in that garden. . . . Experience seeking a treasure . . . whatever it is . . . and somehow, somewhere you will find it. . . . There is a door in one of the walls of the garden. . . . Your eyes keep being drawn to this door. . . . You have a desire to open this door . . . and go through it. . . . The desire grows in you. . . . What is on the other side of this door . . . you keep wondering. . . . What is it you expect to find on the other side? . . . What do you most desire to find on the other side of the wall? . . . Knock on that door . . . or make the effort in some way to go through that door to the other side . . . and experience what you find there. . . .

The power of Jesus made it possible for people to have an actual experience of asking, seeking, knocking through this meditation. His power came from his caring. Each person was helped to have an experience not just of being in a garden but of connecting with deeper desires and spiritual questions within himself. Without this guidance – or the guidance of a spiritual teacher with true caring and power, this meditation–exercise could not achieve its intended aim. This aim is to awaken the asking/seeking part in each one of us.

We cannot grow unless this asking is truly awakened in us. All learning proceeds through asking: asking for material things, asking for knowledge, asking for truth. Some form of asking is always going on in us, even unconsciously, and it draws in many kinds of answers which we are probably not aware of as 'answers'. Until we become aware of our asking – of desires which may contradict each other – we cannot clarify to ourselves what we most deeply want. We need to become aware of the different levels of asking, and especially of those forms which oppose our spiritual asking. Then we need to be able to see the answers which are drawn to us by our own asking – even our unconscious asking. One part of our being asks for growth and a spiritual challenge, and another part asks for security and protection against change. Can we see, and acknowledge, the different things we seek, which contradict each other? Only then can we begin to sort out and evaluate the kinds of asking that are within us.

The universe contains all possibilities for our self-expression and growth. It is both visible and invisible. It is peopled by persons at every level of evolution and distortion who can respond to any level of asking in ourselves. If we 'ask for fish' we will be given fish – but something else in us may ask for a 'serpent', and we will also be given a serpent. If we are truly in a state of spiritual seeking, what we receive will confirm that state and feed us spiritually; but if we are in a state of resentment or jealousy or fear, this state can also receive confirmation. This negative state cannot be removed from us so long as we are secretly seeking its confirmation. It is essential to understand what Jesus was teaching in and through these verses. Otherwise, it is easy to become disenchanted and to develop mistrust towards our spiritual teacher – even towards God – because our states of fear, jealousy, resentment, and so on are not removed for us. What are we asking for? How many things are we asking for? Are we seeking justification for our states? Are we truly seeking to grow beyond these states – which means leaving them behind without justifying them? Can we ask for truth – and truly allow it to be applied to ourselves? Can we seek growth – and trust the One who grows us to the extent of letting go the forms of security that cover up our fears? Can we walk through that door on which we have knocked – and walk through it into a new quality of life that is so different from the smallness of our life now?

No religious structure, no intercessions, no rituals – no prayers, even – can do it for us. There is no magic which can grow us spiritually. Jesus eschewed the use of magic. He gave people experiences of different states in themselves – and of a possible new state of being which they could inhabit; he helped them – he can help us – prepare the ground of themselves so that spiritual growth could take place.

The old mind – the 'old man' in us – cannot be abandoned easily, any more than it can be magicked away by priests or rituals. It has to be carried, like the parcel in the boat, for a long time, by our awareness of it. It will gradually diminish in size and in its effect on our lives *through our consciousness of it*. The carrying of our burden is essential to our own growth and to our increasing ability to help and care for other people. The carrying of those parts of ourselves which have no wish to grow teaches us acceptance – of ourselves and others. It increases patience in us. Our trust begins to grow in the One from whom we ask help in the bearing and sharing of our burden. We learn that we cannot carry our burden alone. This *is* our spiritual growth: the journey with our burden or parcel.

Pass no judgment, and you will not be judged. . . .
(MATTHEW vii, 1-5)

Jesus showed his friends that only by carrying their own
burdens – the burdens of themselves and their weaknesses
– would they be able to help others. This is the kind of
meditation-experience he gave them to illustrate this point.

MEDITATION-EXPERIENCE

Visualise the person whom you find most difficult at this
period in your life. . . . Visualise the person as clearly as you
can. . . . Experience your own reaction to him or her. . . .
Now, experience the corresponding or similar trait in
yourself . . . to the one which you find most difficult in this
person. . . . Face this weakness in yourself as far as you
can . . . and accept its existence without justifying it.
This is the carrying of your own weakness. . . . Now,
carrying your own weakness . . . being aware of it . . .
extend yourself or enter into that person whom you find
most difficult. . . . Allow your passive mind (not the active
mind or intellect) . . . to pick up some new understanding of
that person. . . . Do not put this understanding into words
. . . merely receive the imprint of it on yourself. . . .
Withdraw slowly from the person . . . and return to an
awareness of yourself. . . .

This experience brings with it a different quality of understanding to the one which derives from the above verses.
The commandment 'not to judge' but to look to our own
weaknesses instead cannot produce real, spiritual results. It
creates another kind of hypocrisy in which we do not judge
openly – but carry on with our judgments in secret. They
may even be hidden from ourselves, often because they are
not expressed in so many words but are an attitude of mind.
We are not able wholly to see – let alone remove – the 'plank
in our own eye'. Catching a glimpse of it, we may imagine

that is enough – or we may feel so ashamed that nothing further can take place. It may bury itself again. This is partly through our ignorance: we do not know what to do.

What Jesus taught and gave people practice in experiencing was seeing and accepting. This meant seeing our own weaknesses, but also seeing the weaknesses – often very similar – in other people. It meant also going a step further and *accepting* these weaknesses, both in ourselves and in other people. This was an essential part of his teaching. To accept does not mean to condone; nor does it mean to shrug off with 'This is the way I've always been – and always will!' It means that we accept, as far as we can, the whole of ourselves as we are now, bearing the pain of those parts which are weak or disagreeable or even disgusting. If we can do this with even one unpleasant aspect of ourselves, we can do the same thing with other people and their unpleasant traits.

The ability to see and accept these parts of ourselves comes from a tiny light or spark of truth within us. This spark of light was so increased by Jesus for his friends that they were able not only to see and accept, but also to carry the burden of themselves. Through carrying this burden, in which they were no longer alone, they were able to enter into the other person and not only see, accept – but also help to carry his burden. The shared carrying of our burdens – shared by friend with friend, and shared also with the spirit of Christ – enables them to diminish, slowly but steadily. This is possible for each one of us now.

> He who is not with me is against me, and he who does not gather with me scatters. (MATTHEW xii, 30)

The burden of our weak and recalcitrant self is not only a burden which we simply carry along our spiritual path until such time as it becomes pocket-size or falls off altogether. It is an 'enemy' with which we may have to wrestle; it is a person that stops us in our tracks; it is the part of ourself that 'scatters' the seeds of truth and even sidetracks us from our path. This is the truth – so misunderstood by writer and interpreter – which Jesus found essential to get across to his friends. He was speaking of himself as a Gardener, and he said to his friends: Do you want to grow and use me as your Gardener – or do you not? It was a simple question which needed to be asked many times, not just once. Do we want to grow and use the Gardener? Sometimes we will answer with a profound 'yes'; but sometimes we will experience great resistance in us to change of any kind, but especially to spiritual change that depends upon the help of our Gardener.

Jesus was not referring to any conflict between outside forces: between the 'devil' and 'god'. It was not a question of taking sides. Rather, he was pointing out that there are two sides within each person – within each one of us; there is the side that wants to grow and the side which resists growth. The burden we are carrying contains its own will, and this will can not only resist our desire to grow spiritually but even stop our journey temporarily – but not forever. In the course of day by day living experience with his friends, Jesus showed them the two sides of themselves. Sometimes the side desirous of spiritual growth was uppermost and he could be the Gardener for them. On the other hand, there were times when his friends resisted growth, became frightened and obstinate and wanted to remain as they were. Then Jesus became the 'devil' for them. He had to accept misunderstanding and even calumny. At such times, he helped them to express their resistance to growth – and to himself who represented their growing side – and bore these burdens of themselves. And when again they had returned into that part of themselves which longed for spiritual growth, he reminded them of the opposite part so they could come to know and recognise the two sides of their beings.

Until we can accept and understand these two sides which exist in us, as parts of our own nature, we cannot help other people in any profound way. The spiritual strength required to bear the suffering of rejection or mistrust, as Jesus experienced them at times, can only come through understanding our own natures and experiencing the patience and love of our own Gardener through our times of darkness.

The Journey is not one journey but consists in the many small steps that we take, day by day, and in the new meanings that give encouragement and feed us. These new meanings are like the treasures which children find as they play in the sand pit, or walk along a city street. There is always some thing – a special thing – that transforms the place and the day. It may be a stone, or a nail, or a piece of glass, or a flower in a crack in the pavement. Whatever it is, it becomes the focus for something more than itself; it is, for that child, a window into a tiny piece of eternity.

We, too, need to re-learn how to find 'treasure' in our moments and our days, with each treasure becoming a special 'thing' that lighted up the day and gave it new meaning. The treasure is usually small or slight: a bird poised, a drop of dew, the aroma of steaming earth after rain, but through it we feel the excitement of another dimension entering our life and consciousness. Every day – each hour – has its treasure. All the treasures, taken together, create another kind of pattern in our life. They are like beads strung on the same thread, which is the thread of a deeper awareness. We cannot – and should not – put this into words, but it exists – and they, the treasures, exist – as points of aliveness and growth. These are our 'pearls of great price', leading us, treasure by treasure – as they are strung on the thread of our awakening consciousness, to the one Treasure, the one Pearl of Great Price which we will eventually seek and to which we can commit ourselves with all our heart. This is a simple meditation–exercise which Jesus used to connect his friends with this truth.

MEDITATION–EXPERIENCE

With your creative imagination, visualise your own garden (if you have no garden, visualise a garden familiar to
you). . . . Enter into the garden . . . and look around it. . . .
This garden is you and your life. . . . Observe the different
things that you do in the garden . . . the hard work . . .
digging . . . pruning . . . weeding . . . planting. . . . And
how you could work about in your garden forever in this
way. . . . Or observe your pottering . . . in a desultory
way. . . . Or how you sit in a corner of it and relax. . . .
Experience these activities . . . going on and on. . . .
Observe how it is still the same garden . . . whatever you
do. . . . Observe how plants grow and die . . . and weeds are
weeded and grow again. . . . Observe how the seasons come
and go . . . and come and go again. . . . Suddenly, you find
a treasure in your garden . . . or maybe it just appears. . . .
The treasure you have found transforms the garden . . .
gives it new meaning. . . . Everything is different . . . more
meaningful. . . . Examine the treasure . . . enjoy it. . . .
Allow it to give off a kind of light. . . .

If we ask and seek and knock – and sometimes it may be
without any real awareness that we are doing so, then we
may find at some point in our lives the Pearl of Great Price.
This is more than a garden treasure – more, even, than those
treasures which open our eyes to eternal truths. It
is the treasure our innermost being seeks. Can we recognise it – or does it pass unnoticed? Our lives are so filled
with things and activities and securities – can we sell anything and purchase this Pearl? Can we sell enough of the
possessions that stand in the way of our growing and
commit ourselves to the path and to the teacher who can
guide our steps?

Sometimes the learning experience, in which Jesus involved
his friends, was an actual journey. The lessons derived from

the physical experience. One such journey is recorded in the fourteenth chapter of Matthew.

> Then he made the disciples get into a ship and go on ahead to the other side. After doing that, he went up the hillside to pray alone. It grew late and he was there by himself. The boat was already some furlongs from the shore, battling with a head-wind and a rough sea. Between three and six in the morning he came to them, (*apparently*) walking on the sea. . . . (22–25)

The difficulty with this story, as it is written in the Gospel, is that it involves the use of magic. This is true of many stories and parables in the Gospels, and, as they appear, they cannot be understood as spiritual lessons. Because Jesus rejected the use of magic categorically, these happenings need to be read differently.

Under certain conditions, people can be 'taken back' to the past to experience what in fact took place. This possibility is based on two spiritual facts. One is that the people who were involved in any situation, at whatever point in history, are still alive somewhere in the spiritual universe. The other fact is that events are recorded truthfully on the minds of the participants, regardless of distortions that obscure their perception of things at the time. If truth were not recorded, it would be impossible for learning to take place after the event. From what can be experienced NOW, (this is from my personal experience as a teacher) these appear to be the lessons which the disciples learned from the above-recorded event.

The most important lesson was about *trust*. Jesus had sent the disciples on ahead of himself in a boat, to cross the sea of Galilee. Would he have sent them on this journey to capsize and drown in a rough sea? But *trust* is not faith; it is a relationship between two people and it is based on the experiences they have of each other. Trust is not definitive; it is ever moving; growing, or else dwindling. Growing trust is based on new experiences that provide us with proof that our trust is well-placed. We need always to leap beyond the proof we already have, and in this way our trust grows.

The disciples were in a small boat on a rough sea, with a strong head-wind, and it was night. At night imagination can feed our fears, and we forget what we know spiritually to be true. So Jesus came to them in a vision, at the time of night when they were at their weakest. That is to say, he came to them in his spiritual body, while his physical body was still on the hillside in prayer, and they saw him walking without fear on the rough sea. Their trust in him, and their confidence in themselves, returned.

Then he taught them, further, something that is not recorded in the story. He taught them how to draw always on himself for strength – to draw from him the power of his love to take them through every situation. They did not need to depend upon a 'vision' which he created, but could at any time call on him from their own needs and out of the love and trust they had placed in him; and the response would be immediate. The bond between them – his love for them, their love for him – always existed and could always supply them with the spiritual strength they needed, regardless of whether or not he was physically present. (This was also in preparation for his eventual physical death.)

Then he gave them a meditation-experience.

You are in a small boat on the sea . . . crossing from one side to the other. . . . The wind gets up suddenly . . . and the sea becomes rough. Experience being in the boat on the rough sea. . . . Now, you have a vision of me coming to you . . . walking on the rough seas. . . . It is my spiritual body you see. Experience its calming effect. . . . Consciously draw strength from my spiritual body. . . .

Now, I call to you to come to me . . . over the water. . . . Look into my face . . . and step out of the boat . . . and walk towards me. Experience confidence as long as you look at me. . . . Experience your own ability to walk on the water. . . . Now, you will look away . . . and you will be

The Journey

filled with fear at the roughness of the sea . . . and the
strength of the wind. . . . You will feel that you are going to
sink. . . . I call to you again . . . and you look up. . . . You do
not sink . . . but regain confidence as my strength flows into
you. . . .

Eventually, the wind subsides . . . and the sea becomes
calm. You are back in the boat.

In this simple meditation (which can still be used today),
Jesus took the actual experience which his friends had had
and extended the lesson to show them how it is possible to
walk on top of the circumstances of life, and not sink. There
will always be storms and rough seas in everyone's life, but
we need never sink providing we look up, into the face of
Christ, and draw on his strength. To his friends Jesus gave
an actual experience of these spiritual truths so they would
not forget them. But for every one of us he is spiritually
present and calls to us in the same way: to look on him and,
drawing on his strength, gain the confidence to walk on the
rough seas of our own individual lives.

> At that time the disciples came to Jesus and asked, 'Who is
> the greatest in the Kingdom of Heaven?' He called a child,
> set him in front of them and said, 'I tell you this: unless you
> turn round and become like children, you will never enter
> the kingdom of Heaven'. (MATTHEW xviii, 1-3)

The spiritual journey can only be undertaken by a child.
The childlike qualities in everyone, even if they have
become dormant or atrophied, are the qualities that enable
us to grow spiritually and transcend every barrier or ob-
stacle. These are not qualities that have anything to do with
being humble! They are qualities of an adventurous spirit
and the desire to learn, the quality of acceptance and adap-
tability to circumstance, and – above all – the quality of
trust. The small child – the child in us – goes out to life,
responding to each new thing with curiosity and acceptance
and trust. Its trust means: all will be well, whatever
happens.

Jesus gave his friends an experience of becoming a child

again in connection with both the journey and the up-and-down movement of our boat on the sea, which is caused by our inner obstacles and fears.

MEDITATION-EXPERIENCE

Imagine you are in a very small boat on your own . . . and you are a young child again, of not more than ten. . . . You know without doubt that the boat is quite sure and safe . . . and that it is taking you on a journey. . . . Experience a sense of excitement and adventure. . . .

Now, you are on the sea in your boat. . . . Experience the up-and-down movement caused by the waves and troughs. . . . The movement is gentle to start with. . . .

Suddenly the boat slides into a trough and the waves are high around you. . . . Experience *fear*. . . . Accept the fear as a child would . . . and experience the boat beneath you, shaking but solid. . . .

Now, experience the boat moving up the wave . . . climbing out of the trough . . . and your fear fading. . . .

Experience *strength* growing in you . . . and confidence. . . . You are riding the crest of the wave . . . and moving forward. . . . You are sliding down again into another trough. . . . Experience hopelessness. . . . Face it . . . accept it. . . . Experience a Presence on your boat who manifests in some way . . . and allow yourself to be reassured as a child would. . . . As trust returns . . . you experience the boat moving up the next wave . . . out of the trough. . . .

Now you have some measure of the movement of your boat your excitement returns . . . and your sense of adventure. . . . The boat skims the waves, moving forward on your journey. . . . Again, your boat begins to slide into another trough . . . and you experience childish anger . . . and resentment against the one who directs you on this journey . . . and against this up-and-down movement of the boat. . . . Resistance and obstinacy seem to take over in you . . . and you are cut off from that Presence of whom you

were aware a short time before. . . . Experience this childish
state of resistance. . . . Face this feeling of being cut off . . .
accept it . . . and wait for the boat to start its upward movement. . . . As your boat moves upwards . . . experience a
new emotion . . . which can only be called joy. . . . Let it rise
and absorb you. . . . Experience seeing land ahead . . . and
feel your boat coming closer to the new shore. . . .

Spiritual journeys are never straight lines but grow out
of the kind of undulating movement experienced in this
meditation. Both extremes have to be allowed to happen in
us, the troughs as well as the wave-crests, if the journey is to
take place. We have to experience and become aware of
both extremes in ourselves. Only through allowing ourselves to experience joy, adventuring, trust on the one
hand, and doubts, fear, resistance on the other, can growth
take place. We have to allow ourselves to go into these
different states so that we can experience them consciously
and see *what is* in ourselves. This movement of up-and-
down is part of every spiritual journey a person makes from
one state of being to another. We cannot argue or persuade
ourselves out of fears or doubts; we need to experience
them and know the different sides of ourselves before
change can take place and we can actually arrive on the
new shore. In the meantime, and as our acceptance of the
different manifestations in ourselves grows, the extremes
become less extreme and we become more certain as to the
safety of our boat and the reality of the Presence who
is guiding us on our journey. In fact, our growth takes
place long before we arrive at our destination, for the very
journeying *is* our growth.

3. The Seed

That same day Jesus went out and sat beside the lake, where so many people gathered round him that he had to get into a boat. He sat there, and all the people stood on the shore. He spoke to them in parables, at some length.

He said: 'A sower went out to sow. And as he sowed, some seed fell along the footpath; and the birds came and ate it up. Some seed fell on rocky ground, where it had little soil; it sprouted quickly because it had no depth of earth, but when the sun rose the young corn was scorched, and as it had no root it withered away. Some seed fell among thistles, and the thistles shot up, and choked the corn. And some of the seed fell into good soil, where it bore fruit, yielding a hundredfold or, it might be, sixtyfold or thirtyfold. If you have ears, then hear.'

Jesus used the imagery of boats and the sea and journeys, but also used all the signs and manifestations of nature to show people how growth takes place and to give them experiences of their own growing. Plant life reveals many truths that teach us lessons about ourselves and the nature of our own growing process. Jesus used different aspects and stages of plant life, from seeding to harvesting, to give his friends experiences relevant to their own needs. The above verses illustrate one kind of experience he gave his friends. You are like a piece of ground, he said – only you are not just one piece of ground but several different kinds of ground, some of which are good for planting and others are not. This is how he went on:

MEDITATION–EXPERIENCE

Visualise a piece of ground . . . with a footpath . . . and uncultivated or overgrown parts . . . and some soil that has been well dug. . . . Look at this piece of ground intently with your mind. . . . Now let yourself become this piece of ground. . . . Experience the ground of yourself . . . consisting of different parts. . . . Experience the footpath or wayside in yourself. . . . Experience what happens to thoughts that fall on your footpath. . . . Experience shallow or stony ground in yourself. . . . Experience what happens to thoughts that fall on your shallow ground. . . . Experience the tangled, weedy, undug part in yourself. . . . Experience what happens to thoughts that fall on your tangle of weeds. . . . Experience the rich, well-dug part of yourself . . . and what happens to thoughts that fall on this good soil. . . . Experience these varied parts of yourself . . . and where it is possible for seeds to fall and new growth take place. . . .

If we allow ourselves to have this experience of ourselves, we will find that new growth can only take place in a certain part of our beings. Other parts of ourselves are too busy with many thoughts and other people's opinions. Some parts have shallow soil, where bursts of enthusiasm are possible that wither when they meet resistance in ourselves – or from outside ourselves; they cannot root properly. We need also to experience the stones of our resistance – our literal-mindedness, our obstinacies. And in some parts of our minds there is such confusion of attitude and thought that nothing could possibly grow. Only where the mind has been cleared and space made, where there is depth of soil, can seeds take root and grow properly. We seem to have been born with some soil already prepared, but we need consciously to prepare new places. This meditation, once experienced, goes on working in us and provides us with new insights from time to time.

Another purpose of this meditation, as it was given by Jesus, was to teach his friends how to become more aware of the different kinds of 'soil' in other people and to be sensitive to which state (or 'soil') a person was in, before endeavouring to sow a new idea in his mind. Every exercise that Jesus gave had this twofold purpose of providing self-knowledge and increasing awareness of other people and their states and needs.

The next stage is to plant the seed. Jesus went on with the meditation in this way:

MEDITATION–EXPERIENCE

You are a seed in the ground. . . . Experience being a seed. . . . Experience its smallness . . . the hardness of the shell of protection around you. . . . Enjoy being a seed deep in the earth. . . . Enjoy being snug . . . and safe. . . . Now, experience a force or power working on you . . . causing something in you to vibrate . . . to become excited . . . to want to stretch out beyond the confines of your seed. . . . Experience the response in yourself to this force of creation . . . working on you. . . . Experience also the resistance in yourself to this force . . . to change or growth. . . . Experience your fear of change. . . . Now, allow the force of creation to work on you . . . so that your own desire to grow becomes stronger than the resistance to growth. . . . Experience the softening of the seed-shell . . . and the sending forth of new shoots of growth. . . . Experience pushing up through the soil. . . . Experience obstacles in your way . . . like stones or rocks . . . or predators in the soil. . . . When you encounter difficulties . . . experience more strongly the pull of the light and warmth reaching down to you from above . . . through all the darkness of the earth . . . and drawing you up. . . . Allow yourself to come through the earth at last. . . . Experience the excitement of breaking out into the light. . . . Experience as deeply as you can this entry into a new dimension . . . your joy and tenderness . . . and other emotions. . . . Experience yourself as you breathe in the light and air. . . .

This is a meditation–experience that speaks for itself and will awaken some response in everyone. It makes us more

47

conscious of the growing process in ourselves and of the parts in us that resist growth. As we become more aware of ourselves, so we are better able to understand and help other people with their own particular obstacles.

The growth of the seed is everyone's experience of spiritual awakening. It can happen many times, at different points in our lives, because there are many new beginnings from different aspects of ourselves; there are also many hesitations and stoppings – but no finish line! There are, however, spiritual 'achievements' in the form of reaching that new dimension or level of being as a 'plant', from which return to the seed-state is no longer possible. The plant has become established once and for all. This act of dying to the seed and growing in trust through the darkness of the soil until the surface is reached, and the plant formed, requires different kinds of time-scale. With everyone it is different. It might take years, or weeks – or the growth of a particular 'seed' might even take place for someone during the meditation–exercise itself. There are many seeds in us, and different kinds of plants need to grow in the ground of ourselves before the whole of us can become established in that new dimension of life. This is the essence of Jesus' teaching.

The next meditations are not directly related to the growth of the seed, nor are they about growth into a new dimension or level of being. Jesus gave them originally to his friends as exercises in which they could recognise more easily their own strengths and weaknesses and how they related to the growing process in themselves. They can provide us with detailed experience of what is dead in us or needs to be pruned back, of what is sick or weak, and of the parts that are full of vitality and need more room for expression. These exercises enable us to experience our own personal need for a gardener, without whose help we cannot achieve any of our growth potential.

The Seed

Let the image of a plant come into your mind . . . any kind
of plant that is seeking to grow . . . . Observe the plant
carefully. . . . Now, move up to the plant in your mind . . .
and become the plant. Experience being the plant. . . .
Experience the kind of soil you are in . . . and how it
contains and holds you. . . . Experience also how the soil
restricts you. . . . Experience the kind of garden you are
in. . . . Experience your roots . . . and whether they are
strong and firmly anchored in the soil. . . . Are they inter-
twined with other roots? . . . Experience any other plants
encroaching on you . . . and taking moisture or nourishment from you. . . . Do you need to extend your roots . . .
or put down new roots? Experience your stem and leaf
structure above the ground. . . . Experience the vitality and
growing in you . . . and how it is expressing. . . . Be aware
of any weakness in your own structure that limits your
growth. . . . Is there any sickness? . . . Are there parts that
are overgrown . . . or leggy? . . . Are there any dead parts . . .
or parts that are stunted . . . maybe with mould or some
kind of parasite? . . . Are there parts that need pruning
back? . . . There are also predators of different kinds who
may menace or threaten you. . . . Experience who they are
. . . and what you do in reaction to them. . . . Experience
your reaction to all these challenges . . . that come from
outside you . . . as well as from within yourself. . . .

Not everyone will experience every aspect of this meditation. Sometimes we may need to experience one part of
ourselves, and at another time something else will reveal
itself. Each day is different, and different growths are
possible for us at different times. This is important to
remember with other people.

It is helpful to draw certain parallels between parts of
the meditation and aspects of ourselves or our life. The
plant finds itself in a certain kind of soil, in a particular

garden structure. We find ourselves living within a specific social fabric that belongs to the country and time into which we were born. A specific pattern of thinking and attitude surrounds us and limits us. Other people and many kinds of relationship impinge on our expression of ourselves, and we need to see how we can interfere with one another's growing. We also need to learn how to make our own kinds of growth by putting down new roots and gaining independent strength — and help others to do the same. A plant needs pruning and cutting back so that its vitality can be used for new growth; we can be shown what we have outgrown – attitude or activity – and where we need our own kind of pruning. We can learn where new shoots of growth can begin to bud in us, and where we need healing. The 'predators' that attack the plant may be the challenges or tests that the very nature of our life supplies and which can enable us to grow stronger and overcome some of our weaknesses. But they may also symbolise manifestations of our own self-doubts or gloomy thoughts or emotions that seek to eat into us and destroy the trust and confidence from which we grow.

This meditation is about all kinds of growth – the all-round growth which needs to take place in everyone so that different kinds of intellectual and emotional and physical needs are expressed. Spiritual growth: the growth of our innermost being or will, depends upon this all-round growth in the varied forms of self-expression which make up our nature. This growth is not limited to the moral requirements put upon us by our particular society but includes the *making manifest* of hidden or unpleasant parts of our character as well. We need to allow every part of ourselves to manifest and express in order to strengthen in our will its desire for spiritual growth. But if we are going to allow every part of our nature to express, we need the guidance and caring of a spiritual teacher – and the love of Christ, without whose protection this would be impossible.

This brings us to the next meditation–exercise which

focusses on our need for the kind of help that comes from a spiritual teacher – from someone outside ourselves who has greater insight and compassion and the ability to do things that we are not capable of doing for ourselves. Such is a gardener to a plant. Jesus thought of himself as a gardener, and this is the meditation he gave his friends.

MEDITATION-EXPERIENCE

Visualise a plant . . . any plant, whatever comes to mind. . . . Look at it closely. . . . Touch it. . . . Become the plant. . . . Experience being that plant. . . . Experience clearly your own identity as a plant. . . . Now, experience your needs. . . . Experience your need for nourishment . . . for water . . . for extra space in which to grow. . . . Experience your need for encouragement. . . . Experience any weaknesses in yourself . . . any sickness . . . in your plant. . . . Experience your vulnerability. . . . Now, experience your need for a gardener . . . to protect you . . . to heal your weaknesses . . . to help you become whole. . . . Experience your need for the gardener to encourage you . . . to clear a space around you so that you may grow stronger . . . to feed you. . . . Experience your needs . . . and your helplessness . . . without the gardener. . . . Now, experience the gardener. . . . Let the gardener come up to your plant. . . . Experience also your own mistrust . . . your fear of giving yourself to the gardener. . . . Allow your needs to increase . . . allow your sense of helplessness to grow . . . and overcome your fears and mistrust of the gardener. . . . Now, experience the nourishment . . . the encouragement . . . the healing . . . the protection . . . that come from the gardener. . . . Experience what happens in yourself through the gardener's caring. . . .

This is an important meditation because it enables us clearly to experience our needs and the fact that we are incapable of supplying our own needs. This meditation can show us our helplessness – if we will allow it to do so – and how we depend upon the 'gardener', the person or persons without whom we cannot grow.

In the 'Lord's prayer' meditation, we learn gradually to extend ourselves into the Person – physical or spiritual – whom we accept as our spiritual teacher or master. It takes time – sometimes a long time – and courage to let go the barriers sufficiently, that surround and protect our independent self, to make this meditation possible. The plant meditation above is concerned with a more basic level of everyday living, in which we experience our needs and helplessness in physical terms. The barriers may also be more apparent to us and the question therefore more starkly put, as to whether or not we can give ourself to the gardener. Do we hand over ourself to the care of the gardener, or do we carry on in our under-nourished, partly-grown state? Although we may experience this particular meditation infrequently, this is a question we have to ask ourselves daily. Indeed, it is THE question we eventually need to ask from moment to moment: Do we carry on as we are – or do we seek help from the gardener *now*, at this moment in time, with this particular problem or need or decision? We have to learn from this meditation how difficult it is to ask this question, because upon its asking truly depends our own spiritual growing.

Sometimes we cannot truly ask for help until we are brought low by illness or misfortune of a kind that stops us in our tracks or brings us to the limits of our endurance. A strong will cannot let go; we have to try every path or method for ourselves before we ask for help or guidance. Many of Jesus' friends were like this. Simon Peter appears to have been such a person. If the story is true, he went to the limit of his denial of knowing Jesus – as Saul went to the limit of his persecution of Jesus' followers. And yet, the strong will of each of these men became the bed-rock of certainty and conviction when they had reached the dead end of themselves on one level and finally accepted the enlightenment which led to the new level of spirituality in themselves. Some people struggle with illness and pain until they are exhausted and, becoming passive to their situation, are able to receive spiritual help at last. The one who seeks spiritual growth may also, for a long time, be feeding his desire to do it himself – alone, and without help. The fears may be too strong to accept the 'gardener's' caring. A crisis has to occur in his life before he can leap over these fears in desperate need of help, thereby enabling his new knowledge to be converted into spiritual fact. That conversion in us of knowledge into substance – the journey from one level to another, the growth of the seed – can only be made possible by a spiritual teacher communicating the love of Christ. How long it takes some of us to accept this truth and act on it.

Jesus' friends experienced the intensity of his teaching through his own personal presence. We can experience his spiritual presence – but that is not enough. We also need a physical person as our teacher, whose physical presence can challenge and teach us in a way that is impossible through a solely spiritual relationship. The spiritual growth possible for us during our physical lifetime can only come through direct contact with a spiritual teacher who is also inhabiting a physical body. If we practise the above meditation occasionally, we will become aware that this is so. Our barriers to accepting help from a *physical* person, as distinct from someone on the spiritual plane, readily become apparent to us. It is the contact and relationship between two physical persons that can reveal our barriers to ourselves. Unless – or until – we become aware of these barriers, and carry this awareness with us for a time, we will not be able to accept the very help we need for our growth. A 'gardener' waits for everyone who desires to grow, everywhere in the world, but he – or she – cannot help us until we put ourselves in his hands.

Both of these plant meditations can be used separately to provide different kinds of experience, or they can be given as a series of meditations that, having an inner dynamic, make new growth possible. This may be difficult to understand. But these meditations are not one-off exercises which finish when the person re-directs his consciousness to the physical conditions in which he exists. The particular meditation may carry on yeasting in the person and continue to provide him with experiences, dreams, insights for days or even weeks afterwards. Even more than that, the action of the meditation – growing, being pruned, etc. – can have a direct effect on the person and bring about an actual change in his spiritual being. Jesus used these meditations in this way, and we can also experience in them the power to create us. If they are used by a spiritual teacher today, they may be imbued with power by Christ and work in us in the same way they worked in his friends, two thousand years ago.

The essence of Jesus' teaching is focussed on the change it is possible for us to make in our spiritual centre of gravity. This is a fundamental change in how we think and feel about ourselves and in the purpose around which our lives revolve. This change has to do with *giving* and the place in ourselves from which we give. This change is concerned with the growth of our *heart* as our new centre of gravity. It may be expressed as a gradual shift in emphasis from a head centring to a heart centring.

While we live in our heads, our relationships to other people are determined in large part by 'law': our striving to live up to the moral law of our times and our fear of transgressing it. Our giving is related to some form of compulsion, social or religious. The time comes for everyone – and it may not be in this life on earth – when we have gone as far as we can in our various forms of self-expression in relation to (or in reaction to) the 'law'. The desire grows in us for a new quality of life and expression. Jesus' teaching is focussed on encouraging and guiding every person who has reached this stage in his or her own spiritual evolution.

This next series of meditations has to do with our

experience of giving to other people. Jesus taught that the quality of giving which we experience on the higher level of being – in our heart centre, in the Kingdom of Heaven – is different to what people habitually express in their relationships with one another. It does not come from any striving to live up to an image of 'doing good'. It is not based on custom. It comes solely from a new point of growth in ourselves where we *desire* to respond to the other person's need.

It is most important to state at this point that the new quality of giving, which Jesus' life was to enable in those people who were ready to learn, has nothing to do with *sacrifice*. There is no dichotomy in Jesus' teaching between 'self' and 'other'; the *giving* of self never means the *sacrifice* of self. 'Sacrifice' is an idea which belongs, like all ideas and abstractions, to man's intellect; where a person acts from such an idea or abstraction, he is acting from his head. The level of giving which Jesus made possible in people who were ready for it is centred on the heart. The heart contains no ideas about giving but only the desire – which is our will – to learn to respond to the need of another person.

The desire to respond may exist in us but the journey is a long one, because there are many obstacles in us that stand in the way of giving. These obstacles, attitudes, reservations have to be recognised and accepted so the desire and the ability to respond can increase in us. This is how Jesus taught his friends to see how and what they were able to give and the barriers that stood in the way of their giving.

MEDITATION–EXPERIENCE

Visualise an orchard of fruit trees covered with springtime blossom. . . . Observe the different kinds of fruit trees in this orchard. . . . Go up to one of the trees . . . and become the tree. . . . Experience the growing in yourself . . . in the blossom. . . . Enjoy this expression of growing. . . . Now, experience another kind of desire in you to produce something useful . . . not just an expression of yourself . . . but for others . . . to be given away. . . . Allow fruit to form. . . . Experience the fruit forming . . . your feelings about it. . . . Allow it to ripen. . . . Someone wants to pick some of your fruit. . . . How do you react? . . . Experience the tussle in yourself between holding onto your fruits . . . and letting them drop. . . . Experience the conditions under which you will allow your fruit to be taken. . . . Will you allow someone to pick it? . . . Anyone? . . . Someone special? . . . Or do you alone decide when to drop it? . . . What do you want to do with your fruit? . . . Experience the gradual letting go of your fruit. . . . How do you feel? . . .

Even if we experience this meditation now as a joyous giving of our fruits, on another occasion we would be likely to experience the barriers in ourselves to that giving. The barriers *are* ourself, our own nature; the desire to give as a free action, without conditions, requires a spiritual leap. This is the spiritual leap which Jesus came to make possible through his teaching – but especially through his own giving.* (See Chapter 5) This meditation, and the one which follows on from it, may be practised a number of times, and each time our knowledge grows and, with increasing insight, also our ability to act givingly from the new growing place in ourselves.

Our fruit can stand for different kinds of things that we may give. It may be something we have acquired or something we have produced; it may be an aspect of ourselves. Eventually, we are asked to give ourselves. This is the extended form of the meditation on giving.

MEDITATION-EXPERIENCE

Visualise an orchard with trees that are starting to come into fruit. . . . Focus on one of these trees . . . go up to it in your mind. . . . Become the tree. . . . Experience being the tree. . . . Experience the fruit forming . . . and your feelings

The Seed

about it. . . . Allow it to ripen. . . . Experience what happens to the fruit. . . . Do you give it away? . . . Does someone take it? . . . What conditions do you impose? . . . Experience the gradual letting go of your fruit. . . . How does it feel? . . . Now, slowly withdraw from your tree and stand beside it. . . . Experience someone coming into the orchard . . . and up to you . . . and asking you for help. . . . How do you respond? The person is asking you to share yourself. . . . Experience sharing yourself through physical contact. . . . Experience any barriers in yourself. . . . Experience sharing your mind with this person . . . the overlapping of minds in some way. . . . Experience any mental barriers in yourself. . . . Experience the sharing of your soul . . . if possible a blending or intermingling of souls: of purpose, of direction, of life-force. . . . Withdraw from the experience of sharing. . . . Let the other person move away. . . . Let the orchard slowly fade. . . .

We may respond to someone's need by giving him something we *have*, but still withhold ourselves. We may even appear to be giving ourselves: a hand-shake, a thought, our time – and even so withhold the true giving of ourselves in response to that person's real need. Conventional giving is from the head: what we think the person ought to have, what we are prepared to give, with the conditions that surround our giving. These meditations which Jesus gave his friends were to enable them to experience another kind of giving which belongs to another level of being, called the Kingdom of Heaven. This is the quality of giving which can come from the heart of us, in response to an actual need – not to any idea about giving. To respond to another person's need, whatever it may be, requires great sensitivity on our part. It also requires insight into the conditions we habitually impose on our giving. These may be physical conditions that relate to touching or to the making of physical space in our lives. They may be mental conditions or attitudes that limit the nature of our giving and what we allow to be asked of us. They may be fears that refer to our vulnerability as persons and cause us to hold back our spiritual beings from the contact and the giving which are required. These insights come through experiencing ourselves; the desire to give freely can grow in the same way. This is why Jesus taught people in this way, so that through experiences in awareness – guided by Jesus – they would come gradually to inhabit and live in the Kingdom of Heaven.

When we consider truthfully what it means to give ourself, we realise that the Kingdom of Heaven is a vast country which we cannot occupy all at once and in which we have almost limitless possibilities for growth. We may start to give from our heart, and as we go on giving our heart grows and expands and the giving becomes more simple, and less conditioned. The nature of our giving can grow throughout the whole of our life on earth – and into the next. This is the possibility we experience in these meditations.

What do we receive from all this giving? The part of ourselves that still places conditions on our giving, that holds back from sharing, is the part that asks this question. What are the wages of giving and service? This is how the question is put in the Gospels.

The kingdom of Heaven is like this. There was once a land-owner who went out early one morning to hire labourers for his vineyard; and after agreeing to pay them the usual day's wage he sent them off to work. Going out three hours later he saw some more men standing idle in the market-place. 'Go and join the others in the vineyard,' he said, 'and I will pay you a fair wage'; so off they went. At noon he went out again, and at three in the afternoon, and made the same arrangement as before. An hour before sunset he went out and found another group standing there; so he said to them, 'Why are you standing about like this all day with nothing to do?' 'Because no one has hired us', they replied; so he told them, 'Go and join the others in the vineyard.' When evening fell, the owner of the vineyard said to his

The Seed

steward, 'Call the labourers and give them their pay, beginning with those who came last and ending with the first.' Those who had started work an hour before sunset came forward, and were paid the full day's wage. When it was the turn of the men who had come first, they expected something extra, but were paid the same amount as the others.

(MATTHEW XX, I-II)

Jesus presented this as a learning experience for his friends in the form of a meditation. What are the wages of service? Someone asked. The question may have been motivated by jealousy. Someone new came into the fellowship of close followers around Jesus who responded quickly, giving himself joyously. How could he do it and obviously receive such joy in the giving? Jesus must then have explained how people are at different stages in their own patterns of spiritual growth and could therefore respond more easily – more joyously – from the new place in themselves. Some people were born at a different stage; they had already worked through difficulties that others were facing now. Comparisons are useless. Furthermore, everyone has a different kind of work to do – a different harvest to bring in which could not be compared with anyone else's harvest. This is the meditation-experience he gave his friends.

MEDITATION-EXPERIENCE

Visualise a village that you know . . . where harvesting of some kind is going on. . . . Experience yourself in that village . . . being called on to help with the harvest. . . . Experience the kind of harvest (whether corn . . . fruit . . . potato . . . other) and the activity in which you are engaged. . . . Experience the actual work of harvesting. . . . Now, the harvest field turns into people . . . and you are harvesting people. . . . Experience how you help the people in your field. . . . Experience giving to people . . . and what you give. . . . Experience your harvesting of people. . . .

Experience also what you receive as you give. . . . This is your wage. . . .

Everyone who experiences this meditation exercise may experience joy in harvesting people and a nourishment of that part of themselves from which the giving is expressed. We are fed, when we give from the heart – when we can share even a small portion of ourself, out of all proportion to the giving, the effort, the time. Even if the giving is rejected – which it sometimes is, for that is part of the other person's learning process, we are still nourished and strengthened in our growing part. This must be experienced to be understood – not only in meditations but within the context of our daily life. Jesus teaches and enables us there as well.

4. The Power of Jesus

While he was still speaking, a man came from the president's house with the message, 'Your daughter is dead; trouble the Rabbi no further.' But Jesus heard, and interposed. 'Do not be afraid,' he said; 'only show faith and she will be well again.' On arrival at the house he allowed no one to go in with him except Peter, John, and James, and the child's father and mother. And all were weeping and lamenting for her. He said, 'Weep no more; she is not dead; she is asleep.' But they only laughed at him, well knowing that she was dead. But Jesus took hold of her hand and called her: 'Get up, my child.' Her spirit returned, she stood up immediately, and he told them to give her something to eat.

(LUKE viii, 48–55)

This story illustrates, clearly and simply, the fact of Jesus' power – a power which could call back a spirit that had left its physical body so that it re-entered and the body came to life again. It was a manifestation of great *spiritual* power which contained insight into the purpose of the child's life and the realisation that her spirit still needed to learn from a physical life on earth. Jesus responded simply to the child's need with a power that came from his own being.

This power in Jesus was inherent in the quality of giving himself in response to the needs of other people. This quality of giving had evolved in Jesus to a stage beyond anything we are able to comprehend, and with every giving of himself, in whatever form, went the power that made the giving effectual. Some of the manifestations of that giving and its power we will discuss in this chapter.

We need to understand that as the power of Jesus was contained within the giving of himself, so the giving was related to the need of each individual person, at any one moment in time. The need of the person was understood by Jesus' insight into his or her whole being. He saw the need and the potential together. So, the vision, the giving, the power called back the spirit of Jairus's daughter because she had not completed her learning experience in a physical body. This was enacted in front of the three friends and the parents of the girl because they were capable of learning from the experience.

Every meditation–exercise which Jesus gave contained power, because in each meditation he gave something from himself to the ones who were taking part. Every person's experience therefore contained a spiritual power that could carry on having an effect long after the meditation had apparently been concluded. The effect of this power was to grow and nourish the person spiritually and to help break down the obstacles to his growth. The placing of power within a meditation is shown very clearly in a simple exercise which Jesus often gave to larger groups of people, wherever he was talking about the 'good news of the kingdom of God'. (See Luke iv, 43)

MEDITATION–EXPERIENCE

Visualise a small cell or gaol . . . as clearly as you can. . . . Allow yourself to be confined in this cell. . . . Experience your confinement. . . . Experience the thickness of the walls . . . the iron gate with locks . . . the small window with hardly any vision of sky outside. . . . Experience the lack of air . . . the heaviness. . . . Recognise this as a spiritual state in which you often find yourself. . . . Experience the gaoler who brings you food . . . and locks you up again. . . . The food is quite meagre. . . . Experience the state of depression which overcomes you from time to time in this place. . . . Experience what limited movement you have. . . . Now, experience a light shining in one corner of your cell. . . . Look at the light . . . focus on it. . . . The light grows . . . in brightness and in size . . . until it takes the shape of a person. . . . Experience this person . . . this angel. . . . Allow the person to speak to you. . . . Let him tell you there is no need to remain in this cell any longer. . . . Let him tell you it is a prison of your own making. . . . Let him show you the keys to the gate of your cell . . . which have always been hanging on the wall beside the gate. . . . When the light of the angel has faded . . . take the keys from the wall of your cell . . . put them in the lock . . . and open the gate. . . . Go out of your cell into the daylight . . . and the fresh air . . . and experience your freedom from imprisonment. . . .

The aim of this exercise was to tell people about the Kingdom of Heaven as a place in themselves where they could be free from the prison or bondage into which they had put themselves and which kept them from growing. Even with large groups of people or casual passers by Jesus did not merely talk about the 'good news'; he gave them an experience of themselves as they were and of what was possible for them. They actually experienced their imprisonment and their freedom from bondage. Into the experience which Jesus made it possible for people to have, he put his power; this power transformed it from a simple, one-off experience into a spiritual action which could carry on within the person for a long period of time. In this particular meditation, the power of Jesus focussed on the person (or angel) and the keys which had always been hanging on the wall. The meditation–experience showed people how to use the keys and opened them spiritually to the power of Jesus. This power had the effect of releasing them temporarily from their prison–cell or bondage. The process of becoming free had begun, and the person's will to grow was encouraged. The power would continue to act within each person, long after the meditation was concluded, but its effectiveness would depend upon the individual's own personal response, from day to day.

> . . . everyone in the crowd was trying to touch him, because power went out from him . . . (LUKE vi, 19)

Wherever Jesus went in his physical body, his spiritual

being went with him, giving out caring and power to
people who were aware of their needs and also to those
who were not. Some people actually touched him because
they knew intuitively they would receive something from
him, and they were aware of the power that came into
them. The experience of this power was in relation to
their needs. It was like electricity, or like warmth; it was
an enlightenment or it was an assurance; it was a lifting
of burdens or fears; it was even a physical healing. Most
often, the physical results followed in time from the spiritual experience.

The spiritual being of Jesus was always giving out caring
and power, wherever he was and whether or not he was
aware of it himself. Sometimes his consciousness was
focussed on what he was saying to a group of people while
his spiritual being was occupied in its own way; but he was
always aware of the giving out of power when someone
touched him – not because he experienced any diminishment but because their need touched his awareness.

So it is with all of us, whatever the spiritual level on which
we are living. Wherever we move in our physical bodies,
our spiritual beings give out their vibrations. They may
emit fear and tension rather than caring, because we are
afraid of our sensitivities and hold back from giving. But
they can give out what is within them to give – if we
allow it.

'Who is my mother? Who are my brothers?' And looking
round at those who were sitting in the circle about him, he
said, 'Here are my mother and my brothers. Whoever does
the will of God is my brother, my sister, my mother.'
(MARK iii, 34-5)

He left that place and went to his home town accompanied
by his disciples. When the Sabbath came he began to teach
in the synagogue; and the large congregation who heard
him were amazed and said, 'Where does he get it from?' and,
'What wisdom is this that has been given him?' and, 'How
does he work such miracles? Is not this the carpenter, the

son of Mary, the brother of James and Joseph and Judas and Simon? And are not his sisters here with us?' So they fell foul of him. Jesus said to them, 'A prophet will always be held in honour except in his home town, and among his kinsmen and family.' (MARK vi, 1-4)

Jesus used the image of the family many times to symbolise a group of people, closely connected with one another through bonds of caring. Jewish society and religion are based on the closely-knit blood relationship of the family – caring, but often rigid as far as its individual members are concerned. It was the image of mutual caring – the fellowship of persons of all ages and both sexes, who desired to 'do the will of God', which he referred to as 'family'. All the people – all the so-called 'strangers' and 'outsiders' – even Galileans – who desired to grow spiritually, who were aware of their needs, who asked for help in becoming free of their prisons, who asked for teaching – they were his family. The ones who listened were his family. Even the ones who, although unconscious of who he was, received power from him because they knew their need, were his 'mother and his sister'.

The biological family unit is held together by the society's requirements for stability and the religion's ethics that inflict punishment and guilt for transgression, more than by mutual caring. Very often members of the blood family cannot accept who its individual members are; they cannot see beyond the physical covering of the person. Jesus showed how in his own town, where people thought of him only in relation to his family background, no one could receive help from him.

This was a many-sided lesson he was teaching his friends. He was teaching them how to transcend the limitations of their own family units and extend their awareness and caring to other people. He was showing them what real caring was and the quality of responsibility for other people which developed into a real family. His power was here the power of light and truth that could show them how the family, as a social unit, could not accept him – could not accept them as spiritually growing individuals. But the power of his own caring, in his concourse with those of his friends who were daily in his presence, gave them an experience of what a true family was like.

The power of Jesus gave people not only the light to see truth but also the strength to become less afraid of transgressing social requirements and family expectations, to lose some of their feelings of guilt, to become able to listen to their own growing individuality.

In small groups of two or three at a time, Jesus gave his close friends the experience of seeing the broad spectrum of themselves as if they consisted of a collection of separate individuals. This brief but profound meditation was only possible with those of his friends who truly desired the truth about themselves and could therefore allow his power to reveal it to them. This is the simple meditation-structure he used.

After you have relaxed your body and your mind as far as you can . . . and offered your mind to the light of truth . . . You will allow yourself to be raised up . . . out of your body awareness . . . along with me and my presence . . . And we will come to rest above where our physical bodies are sitting. . . . Look down on your body where it is sitting . . . and you will see not one body . . . but several bodies resembling you . . . but in fact different aspects of yourself. . . . Observe these bodies . . . these manifestations of YOU carefully. . . . Observe the manifestations of you that hold you back from your journey . . . your growing. . . . Observe what they want instead . . . for themselves. . . . Ask for increased light or guidance to see clearly who they are in yourself. . . . Observe clearly the YOU with whom you identify as the growing part of yourself . . . and see how this YOU differs from the others. . . . Now, return slowly to an awareness of your physical body. . . .

The success, or otherwise, of this exercise always depends upon the extent to which the individual person is ready to receive truth about himself, and upon his need at that particular moment in time. A woman, suffering recently from mental inertia and physical fatigue, saw seven selves sitting in a row, dressed like herself but with different attitudes and shapes. Only one of these was important to observe clearly at that moment. This was a baby that wanted only to sleep or be entertained. The woman regained her energy and mental alertness very quickly after this meditation. A young man, who had recently come to near-suicide, saw three people poaching on himself. All four were dressed in his clothes. One was a baby who sought attention; the second was a self-centred, self-indulgent adolescent; the third was a thin man who whispered doubts and depressing thoughts in his ear. When he had experienced what he had taken to be his own depressing thoughts as those of the thin man whispering in his ear, the young man felt new strength flowing into him. The whispering became fainter.

These are contemporary experiences of the meditation which Jesus used nearly two thousand years ago to enable people at a certain stage to see different aspects of themselves as separate individuals, occupying the same body. This exercise makes it possible for a person gradually to withdraw energy from the different 'people' who are inhabiting his being and blocking his growth. For his friends, Jesus provided the power that made their experiences possible; they needed to continue to call on that power as they returned, again and again, to their own particular vision of themselves. This power was always present – but they needed to call on it and use it if they wanted to strengthen their own spiritual identity. And so it is with us today.

I am the real vine, and my Father is the gardener. Every barren branch of mine he cuts away; and every fruiting branch he cleans, to make it more fruitful still. You have already been cleansed by the word that I spoke to you.

> Dwell in me, as I in you. No branch can bear fruit by itself,
> but only if it remains united with the vine; no more can
> you bear fruit, unless you remain united with me.
>
> (JOHN XV, 1-4)

Just as natural energy and sap flow through all the branches
of the vine, so does spiritual power flow through us if we do
not isolate ourselves. As the plant holds itself in readiness
for the gardener to prune and make more fruitful, so does
our growth and fruitfulness depend upon our own spiritual
gardener. The effectiveness of Jesus' power in the individual
person depends upon his or her acceptance of him as the
Gardener and upon being accessible to that power, and not
isolated.

It is easy to think of the hermit as an extreme form of
physical isolation and the state of depression as the extreme
of spiritual isolation. We then overlook our own kinds of
isolation, whereby parts of ourselves are cut off from the
spiritual whole and can stagnate or become overgrown
without our knowing it, until they begin to take over or
damage the whole of us. Jesus likened ourselves – our beings
– to a field or a garden, each part of which needed our
attention and to be worked on at some time or other. In
this way, no aspect of ourselves would be overlooked or
become isolated from the whole, but every part of us would
be capable of expression, growth, fruitfulness. This is the
form of meditation–experience he gave his friends to enable
them to see the different parts of themselves and the kind of
work needed to be undertaken by themselves with the help
of the gardener.

MEDITATION-EXPERIENCE

Visualise a garden. . . . Now, enter into . . . and experience
being in that garden. . . . Get the sensation of your feet
standing on the ground . . . or the grass . . . or on a path. . . .
Experience the air of the garden. . . . First of all, you walk
around the whole of your garden . . . to see how things

are . . . what the different plants are doing. . . . You look at
the beds of flowers . . . and enjoy how they have grown. . . .
You look at the shrubs . . . and bushes . . . and any fruit-
producing trees. . . . You find a small group of trees . . . and
look at one tree in particular. . . . There is a pond or small
lake nearby . . . and you listen to the sound of a stream
which flows through the garden into the pond. . . . You are
aware of bird life . . . and maybe animal life . . . inhabiting
this part of the garden. . . . You walk on . . . and there is an
area of cultivated grass or lawn. . . . Beyond the lawn is an
isolated patch – maybe quite a large area of waste ground,
with brambles and nettles and coarse undergrowth. . . .
There is no path to this place. . . . You may find a green-
house . . . if you look for it . . . or place for bringing on
special plants. . . . And there may be a summer house . . . for
people to sit in and enjoy the garden. . . . When you have
walked around your garden and looked at it . . . you stand
and feel the whole extent of it. . . . It is *your* garden . . . every
part of it. . . . It is you . . . yourself. . . . Now, you have the
feeling that some kind of work is needed in your garden. . . .
Maybe you have seen many things that need attending
to. . . . You cannot work without a gardener . . . who has
skills beyond your knowledge . . . and abilities you do not
have. . . . He also has tools to lend you . . . and he will guide
you in the using of them. . . . Allow the gardener who tends
this garden to approach you. . . . Be aware of his presence in
some way . . . even if you cannot see him clearly. . . . Let the
gardener take you to a flower bed . . . where there are dead
heads that need removing. . . . Begin the work of removing
these dead heads . . . under his instruction. . . . Ask the
gardener to tell you what they mean . . . these dead heads in
yourself. . . . Now, let the gardener take you to some shrubs
or bushes that need pruning back . . . to increase their
strength and growing power. . . . Let him give you the
tools . . . and instruct you in pruning one of the shrubs or
bushes. . . . Ask the gardener to show you what these parts
correspond to in yourself . . . that need to be pruned. . . .

Finally, let the gardener take you to a tree that needs to be attended to. . . . Maybe there is a dead branch that needs removing. . . . Let the gardener help you . . . and do what you can do. . . . What you cannot do yourself . . . ask the gardener to do. . . . Now, let the garden and the gardener slowly fade . . . and your consciousness return to your physical body. . . .

This is a specifically on-going meditation to which the person who has experienced it returns, again and again, continuing with the work of removing dead heads, pruning, cutting out dead wood. As the meditation progresses, he will be given clearer insight into the parallels with himself and his own mind. In time, he will become aware of a kind of mental pruning having taken place in himself and the gradual disappearance of even deep-seated attitudes or fears that are dead – which he has outgrown. It may happen quite rapidly. After a period of time, which should not exceed three weeks, the person needs to be guided once more through the same meditation-exercise, in which he is taken – not around the whole garden – to another kind of activity, such as weeding or clearing waste ground, with another correspondence to his spiritual being or mind. And, as he repeats the activity on his own, every few days, working physically in his imagination, so there will be a corresponding clearance or removal of obstacles on the mental plane in himself. In this way the above meditation can be used for more than half a year to bring about rapid spiritual changes in the person or persons concerned.

The gardener in the meditation was – and is – for each person the focus for the power of Jesus. The spiritual body of Jesus manifested as the gardener in the meditation of each person to whom he gave the meditation and in that person's private on-going meditation, giving him instruction in what was needed and insight into the related spiritual problem. This is still possible for people who are taken through this meditation today. The power of Jesus works on the spiritual plane through the agency of the gardener, while the person works physically in his meditation garden. When the will of the individual person is actively engaged in this exercise, many spiritual changes can be accomplished – often quite miraculously.

When we consider Jesus' methods of teaching and the way in which he made possible the spiritual growth of men and women, from his own caring and power, we could re-write the above verses from the Gospel according to St. John in the following manner:

> Jesus said: 'I am the gardener – you are like the vines in a vineyard. If you will let me, I will cut away every barren branch to make it more fruitful still. But you cannot bear fruit in isolation. Your growth depends on the gardener, that is, on your unconditional acceptance of the gardener's help.'

> In truth, in very truth, I tell you a grain of wheat remains a solitary grain unless it falls into the ground and dies; but if it dies, it bears a rich harvest.' (JOHN xii, 24)

This chapter commenced with the power of Jesus making possible the coming to life again of Jairus' daughter, whose spirit had not completed her sojourn in a physical body. It concludes with showing how that same power can make it possible for us to die to ourselves on one level and to show forth an enriched quality of ourselves on another level. It might mean dying to an obstinacy and wilfulness which prevent our search for Truth and discovering that this same obstinacy has become the quality of endurance and strength we need for our spiritual life. A quality or attitude which is a stumbling block on one level becomes an asset – and more than an asset – at another point on our spiritual path. If we can die to its negative manifestation, it may be reaped as a positive good.

After they had prepared themselves over a certain period of time, Jesus' friends were ready to make the journey which involved dying to themselves in certain respects –

and reaping the harvest of themselves. This is the kind of meditation-journey he took them on.

Start at your home . . . being aware of your own home . . . the things and material possessions in your home . . . the activities of your home. . . . Be aware of the background of your home . . . as impressions of other homes you have had . . . going back to your childhood home. . . . Be aware of the people who belong in your home . . . and the shadowy figures of all the family in your life. . . . even to childhood. . . . Experience all this around you. . . . Bring it with you . . . and bring with you also in your mind everything you enjoy or that makes your life possible. . . . Bring all this with you on your journey . . . and experience yourself with all this . . . and your whole life as you are. . . . You are travelling through space . . . and you land somewhere . . . in a distant country . . . and come to a large stone gate through which you must go if you are to proceed. . . . The gate is covered with many mirrors . . . in which you observe yourself . . . and the many things to which you are attached . . . which are like hooks into you. . . . You need to travel lighter. . . . Unhook what you can from yourself . . . and ask for help if you need it . . . to see more clearly your attachments or to unhook yourself. . . . When you have done what is possible . . . look around to see if any one else needs your help before you go through the gate. On the other side of the gate you will find a garden which will nourish you with an intermingling of colour . . . and sound . . . and perfume. . . .

Now, you continue on your way . . . much lighter . . . and eventually you arrive at a second gate. In order to go through this gate . . . you have to let go . . . or be taken from you . . . your imagination in the form of ideals and expectations . . . what you think you are aiming for . . . what you think you want to live up to . . . or become. . . .

There are spiritual beings at this gate . . . to whom you can offer yourself: your mind . . . and allow the forms of imagination and striving to be pulled from you (like ropes of spaghetti or string) . . . and room is made for real growth. . . . When all you will allow has been taken from you . . . go through the gate. . . . And your thirst will be quenched by pure spring water. . . . You go on . . . and eventually you arrive at the third gate. . . . Looking through this gate you see mountains . . . vast, shining in the distance. . . . Experience excitement at seeing these mountains. . . . Experience fear. . . . Allow yourself to experience all your fears of the unknown. . . . Experience the trembling and paralysis brought on by fear . . . of the unknown . . . of the unpredictable. . . . There appears to be no one at the gate . . . but you are drawn towards it. . . . If you desire to continue your journey to the mountains . . . trust that all will be well and that you are not really alone . . . and walk through the gate. . . . As you walk you will find the fears are being sucked out of you . . . as if from an invisible and loving power. . . . And you will be nourished with spiritual food . . . by unseen hands . . . which will give you confidence and strength. . . . As you go on the mountains seem closer . . . and more alive and challenging . . . drawing you on. . . . The air is clear and the colours more vivid, and there is a sense of vibrancy. . . . You arrive at a fourth gate.

At a certain point . . . at this gate . . . you must go on alone for a time . . . in order to become strong enough to undertake the new responsibilities which belong to your growth of being. . . . Until you can go through this gate . . . you cannot enter into the fullness and wholeness of the self which belongs to you. . . . At this gate become aware of the one relationship to which you are most attached. . . . Experience your attachment . . . your dependence. . . . See the *form* of that relationship to which you are so strongly attached as a kind of *clothing* of the relationship . . . underneath which the true relationship exists. . . . At the entrance to this gate you will find a gentle spiritual being . . . an angel perhaps . . . who will help you remove the *clothing* in which your relationship is covered . . . so that you can pass on naked through the gate. . . .

When you have come through the gate . . . experience being bathed in a pool of strength-giving water . . . and resting on green grass beside the pool. . . . You now move freely . . . up the foothills of the mountains . . . with springing step . . . and being taught continuously, from within yourself, about the nature of all you see . . . and about the meaning and purpose of all life. . . . Experience the freedom . . . and the joy . . . in the continuous communication with your environment . . . and with the voices who are around you . . . although you appear to be alone. . . . You arrive at the last gate . . . which is of luminous white stone. . . . You look through the gate and see people in robes moving about . . . and other people in sick or distorted or crippled states being helped and ministered to by the ones in robes. . . . There is a light and a radiancy over everyone . . . and the power of caring sends forth a vibration which you can even feel where you are. . . . Are you moved at this gate to let go your aloneness . . . and the desires and conditions you have set for your own spiritual growth . . . and enter into this fellowship of helping others? . . . If you are so moved . . . but deeply moved . . . let fall away from you your independence . . . and the separateness of your independence . . . and go through the gate into the light . . . and experience the unspeakable joy and fulfilment in the service of caring. . . .

The power of Jesus expressed – and expresses – in relationships. The guided meditation is a spiritual exercise which is based on the relationship between the teacher and each one of his pupils. The aliveness of any meditation, and the experience possible for any of the participants, cannot be conveyed in words on paper. Words are shadowy things which cannot convey the intensity or the power contained in one of these meditations. The reader will have to take my word – or the word of someone who has actually experienced these meditations, because their full impact will not come across in the reading of this book. But the seeker after Truth will find and draw to himself – or herself – what he seeks, if his search has persistence. The reader who truly seeks will need to read what he can, and take what he can, from the signposts offered in this book and continue with the spiritual effort we all must make, if we are to draw in the power of Jesus to grow us.

5. The Substance of Life

In the fifteenth chapter of St. Matthew's Gospel – as well as in several other places – the story of an actual event is told in which Jesus is supposed to have fed thousands of people on a few loaves and several small fishes. Not only did he feed them with sufficient food for their immediate physical needs, but there was food left over as well.

> Jesus called his disciples and said to them, 'I feel sorry for all these people; they have been with me now for three days and have nothing to eat. I do not want to send them away unfed; they might turn faint on the way.' The disciples replied, 'Where in this lonely place can we find bread enough to feed such a crowd?' 'How many loaves have you?' Jesus asked. 'Seven,' they replied 'and there are a few small fishes.' So he ordered the people to sit down on the ground; then he took the seven loaves and the fishes, and giving thanks to God he broke them and gave to the disciples, and the disciples gave to the people. They all ate to their hearts' content; and the scraps left over, which they picked up, were enough to fill seven baskets. (32-38)

There are different ways of understanding this event. It is most commonly presented as a 'miracle' in which a small amount of food was multiplied so astronomically that it could feed many thousands of people. This is an interpretation of the happening which resembles the 'devil's' temptation to turn stones into bread. If it were the true understanding of what Jesus did, it is not far removed from the 'miracles' performed by magicians of every race, in every culture in the world since the dawn of history. The same kind of magic can still be used today to produce physical phenomena and manifestations.

If you, the reader, have connected with what is recorded in this book – which is grounded in my own experiences of

Jesus' teaching – you will know that this interpretation does not do justice to Jesus and what you have experienced here as the purpose of his life on earth. You will see the inadequacy of such a materialistic interpretation, and you will understand that magic – and this is in fact what it would have been – could not have opened people's minds to the existence of a *spiritual* reality. And this was the purpose in every aspect of Jesus' teachings: to demonstrate and enable people to experience the actual existence of a spiritual reality.

Jesus had been helping the thousands of people on the hillside for many hours – in this account for three days. His help – his giving – was always of a spiritual nature, even when physical healing was involved. After such a long period of time with Jesus, and being fed spiritually, the people were naturally hungry and needed physical food. This was the climax of their time with Jesus, for which he had been preparing them all along. Now he could demonstrate, in a lesson they would never forget, that what he had been feeding them spiritually could feed them physically as well. Every person present – man, woman, child – received a minute quantity of physical food which, to his astonishment, nourished his body and satisfied his immediate physical needs. This was the miracle. The crumb of bread – or fish – was able to satisfy each individual's physical hunger. How could that be? How could a crumb of bread produce the effect of a meal? What did that crumb contain? This was the experience, which every individual person must have had on that hillside, that enabled him to accept the existence of an invisible substance which could enter into them and produce tangible, physical results. This was what we would call today a 'mind-blowing' experience!

The only possible explanation of the accounts of mass feeding, recorded in all the Gospels, is that Jesus placed in each particle of physical food a spiritual substance which not only nourished the person spiritually but physically as well.

This must have been the mind-blowing experience which people had – as it would have been also for ourselves an astonishing miracle, that would lead us to ask many questions.

> God loved the world so much that he gave his only Son, that everyone who has faith in him may not die but have eternal life. It was not to judge the world that God sent his Son into the world, but that through him the world might be saved. (JOHN iii, 16, 17)

God gave his Son – but the son gave himself. This giving of himself was at the core of Jesus' teaching. He gave himself through his power, contained in the spiritual lessons he enabled people to have and in his healings. He also gave himself through the actual substance of his own life and spiritual body. His teaching was – and is – grounded in learning to give ourself. But the giving of Jesus – the giving of ourself – did not mean sacrifice or a giving up of himself.

The idea that to give ourself means to give *up* ourself – the idea that to give ourself to others means a diminishment of self – is a materialistic concept. No story in the Gospels, whether true or untrue, reveals a Jesus that was diminished by giving. On the physical or material plane, things are measured and weighed and judged; to give means to take from one and add to another. But on the spiritual plane, a different quality of life altogether is possible. It is this new and different quality of life which Jesus came to demonstrate as possible for everyone who wanted it – or was ready for it.

Giving is part of this new – or other – quality of life; it is the essence of it. Giving from the heart does not diminish the giver. The giving of Jesus was part of the very texture of his everyday life, it did not manifest only on special occasions. Every time he broke bread with his friends he placed in each portion that substance which he contained in himself, which was of himself, and which was his to give.

The giving did not diminish the substance within him: it was irreducible.

Jesus' own acts of giving were an integral part of his teaching. His giving of himself was always a demonstration of what was also possible for his friends – for other people as well. Everyone of us can learn to live from that part of ourself which can give. Everyone of us can give the power that is in us to give, to encourage other people. Everyone of us can in time learn to give ourself and our life, in some measure – learn to share ourself and experience not a diminishment but an increase in self.

> In truth, in very truth I tell you, unless you eat the flesh of the Son of Man and drink his blood you can have no life in you. Whoever eats my flesh and drinks my blood possesses eternal life, and I will raise him up on the last day. My flesh is real food; my blood is real drink. Whoever eats my flesh and drinks my blood dwells continually in me and I dwell in him.' (JOHN vi, 53–6)

Jesus' teaching, if it was a true teaching that came from the highest spiritual plane, must be consistent in itself and consonant with its overall purpose. No part of it can be inconsistent with that purpose, let alone be contrary to it. Any kind of materialistic interpretation and any explanation which sees in spiritual miracles a demonstration of magic, or a solely physical manifestation, must be a false understanding of Jesus' teaching.

The 'flesh and blood' of Jesus cannot be understood materialistically, as the flesh and blood of his physical body, but must refer to the spiritual substance and power contained within himself, of which his spiritual body was composed. This was the living substance of his own spiritual nature, with which he nourished people spiritually, in his daily concourse with friends and on special occasions. It was also the 'living water' with which he quenched their thirst and which he gave out continuously as the enabling power that made possible spiritual experience, spiritual healing, and spiritual transformation.

If we experience and pray the 'Lord's prayer', as Jesus taught it, we ask for the spiritual food to nourish the new growing part of ourself. When we commence our spiritual journey, our understanding is limited of what this spiritual food is. As our experience of the 'journey' deepens and our spiritual growing takes on a clearer form, we depend increasingly on the spiritual 'meat and drink' to which Jesus referred. The reality of its existence becomes stronger because our need is greater. We experience the inner nourishment – and even, at times, the nourishment of our physical body as well. We experience also the vibration of a spiritual power that enables us to carry on with the journey. Doubts come – they always will – but they can be answered by our own individual experience of the fact of a spiritual reality.